WALKING THE LINE

A CURIOUS WALKER'S GUIDE TO THE FORMARTINE AND BUCHAN WAY

JANET M MCLEMAN

Published by the
Great North of Scotland Railway Association

A reminder that the weather in Buchan can turn nasty. The railway was often blocked by winter snow which blew across the land and lodged in any cuttings it could find. When snowploughs failed, all that could be done was to dig it out by hand, as here near Newmachar in January 1960.

© Janet McLeman 2016
ISBN: 978-0902343-28-3

Published by the Great North of Scotland Railway Association, www.gnsra.org.uk
Printed by **Berforts Information Press, Eynsham, Oxfordshire, OX29 4JB**

Contents

Railways had to erect posts every quarter of a mile showing the distance from the starting point. This was used to calculate fares and freight rates, as they were based on distance. The Buchan lines were measured from Aberdeen. The number shows the miles and the dots the number of quarter miles, so this is the post at 33¾ miles from Aberdeen, just beyond Maud. A few of these posts survive on the Formartine and Buchan Way.

(Front Cover) The Formartine and Buchan Way provides an ideal means to explore the Buchan countryside. It is an easy track to use, whether for a short stroll or a long walk. Much of it has a tarred surface, but parts, such as in this cutting near Strichen, have a compacted stone surface.

(Right) This photograph of the same cutting was taken in August 1953.
(John A N Emslie)

(Above) Maud was an important point on the railway in Buchan. Here trains from Aberdeen divided; one part went to Peterhead and the other to Fraserburgh. By the time this photograph was taken in 1963, that practice had ceased and Peterhead passengers had to change trains. A Peterhead train has arrived on the right and the locomotive is about to run round its coaches ready to return. The photographer was travelling on the train from Fraserburgh. The station building can be seen in the background.

(G N Turnbull)

(Below) Today, the Formartine and Buchan Way still divides here. The station building has been retained and part of it houses a railway museum which is run by a voluntary group. Picnic tables now adorn the platform where once passengers thronged. Notice how many more trees now surround the site.

(Keith Fenwick)

Introduction

The railway mania which hit Great Britain in the Victorian era led to the publication of a plethora of enthusiastic railway guide books of which Bradshaw's *Descriptive Railway Handbook of Great Britain and Northern Ireland* has become the best known.

Similar books published locally described the railway in North East Scotland. One of these, *The Howes o' Buchan, being notes, local, historical and antiquarian, regarding the various places of interest along the route of the Buchan Railway* by William Anderson which appeared in 1865 was the inspiration for this book.

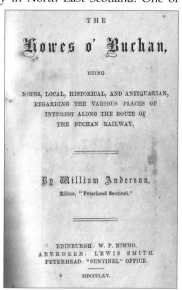

Like similar publications, *The Howes o' Buchan* is a delightfully, quirky guide describing points of interest along the route and on digressions within reach of the stations. *Walking the Line* is intended to provide a similar contemporary guide to what is now the Formartine and Buchan Way – the easily accessible long distance path and cycle route which follows the former railway linking Peterhead and Fraserburgh (locally known as 'The Broch') with Dyce. In all, it extends to 54 miles.

The route is covered by two Ordnance Survey Explorer Series maps; sheet 421 Ellon and Inverurie shows the southern section whilst sheet 427 Peterhead and Fraserburgh includes the north. Points of interest are identified in the book by use of 6 figure OS grid references; for settlements and large features the reference is to a central point.

Acknowledgements

History is not so much memory as collective evidence. It is what has happened, what is thought to have happened, what some claim to have happened. The collective past is fact and fabrication, received truth with just a tenuous thread of events amid a swirl of dispute and collective interpretation.

Penelope Lively, *Ammonites and Leaping Fish : A Life in Time,* 2013

Researching local history is often fraught with difficulty: there are frequently widely differing accounts of what appear to be the most straightforward and well documented events, I hope that I have teased out the most likely solutions to these historical conundrums. In doing so I am indebted to Ian Bain, Charles Burnett, Alison Butcher, Keith Jones, Andrew Kellock, Hon Mrs Kate Nicolson, Loraine Noble, Lady Saltoun, Alan Watson, George Clark, M A Harper, Coleshill Auxiliary Research Team and the Staff of Aberdeenshire Library Service, especially at Fraserburgh Library, for sharing their expertise and advice.

I am also grateful to the many friends, they know who they are, without whose support and encouragement *Walking the Line* would never have been completed. Particular thanks are due to Kath Hamper who provided the superb map, to Alan Stewart of Cabro Aviation Ltd. for providing the excellent aerial photographs and to Keith Fenwick of the Great North of Scotland Railway Association for the history of the railway and for patiently pulling the threads together to prepare the book for publication. Finally thanks to my husband Mike and to Rufus for having walked every step of the way with me – the one metaphorically, the other physically.

All photographs were taken by the author between 2012 and 2015 except where credited.

GREAT NORTH OF SCOTLAND RAILWAY.

FORMARTINE AND BUCHAN SECTION.

OPENING OF FRASERBURGH EXTENSION FOR TRAFFIC.

REDUCTION OF PASSENGER FARES.

On MONDAY, 24th April 1865, and until further notice, Trains will arrive and depart as under :—

DOWN TRAINS—TO FRASERBURGH, PETERHEAD, &c.

STATIONS.	Pass 1 & 3	Pass 1 & 3	Pass 1 & 3	Pass 1 & 3	Pass Par. 1 & 3	Pass 1 & 3	Pass 1 & 3	Pass 1 & 3
	A.M.	A.M.	A.M.	P.M.	P.M.	P.M.	P.M.	P.M.
Aberdeen, depart ...	...	6·20	8·40	...	1·50	3·0	Fridays and Saturdays only.	6·0
Kittybrewster... ...	...	6·29	8·48	...	1·58	3·7		6·8
Woodside	...	6·33	8·52	...	2·2	3·11		6·12
Buxburn	...	6·39	8·59	...	2·9	3·16		6·17
Dyce Junction arrive	...	6·46	9·12	...	2·16	3·22		6·23
Dyce Junction depart	...	6·50	9·16	...	2·20	3·24		6·25
Parkhill...	...	6·54	9·20	...	2·24	3·29		6·29
New Machar	...	7·7	9·32	...	2·38	3·41		6·44
Udny	...	7·16	9·41	...	2·47	3·50		6·55
Logierieve	...	7·20	9·45	...	2·51	3·54		6·59
Esslemont	...	7·25	9·50	...	2·56	3·59		7 4
Ellon	...	7·35	9·55	...	3·5	4·5		7·12
Arnage	...	7·46	10·5	...	3·17	...		7·25
Auchnagatt	...	7·57	10·16	...	3·30	...		7·37
New Maud Junct. ar. (Formerly Brucklay.)	...	8·12	10·30	...	3·45	...		7·50
New Maud Junct. dep.	7·10	8·15	10·33	...	3·50	Fridays & Saturdays only.	6·10	7·53
Old Deer & Mintlaw	7·22	8·26	10·45	...	4·5		6·21	8·5
Longside	7·32	8·36	10·55	...	4·15		6·30	8·14
New Seat	7·37	8·40	10·59	...	4·21		6·34	8·18
Inverugie	7·45	8·45	11·5	...	4·26		6·40	8·25
Peterhead arrive ...	7·55	8·55	11·15	...	4·35		6·50	8·35
New Maud Junct. dep.	7·5	...	10·33	1·15	3·50		...	7·53
Brucklay	7·10	...	10·36	1·19	3·54		...	7·57
Strichen	7·26	...	10·48	1·31	4·6		...	8·10
Mormond	7·36	...	10·56	1·39	4·14		...	8·18
Lonmay	7·46	...	11·2	1·47	4·21		...	8·25
Rathen	7·54	...	11·10	1·56	4·28		...	8·32
Fraserburgh arrive ...	8·10	...	11·25	2·10	4·40		...	8·45

UP TRAINS—FROM PETERHEAD, FRASERBURGH, &c.

STATIONS.	Pass 1 & 3	Pass Par. 1 & 3	Pass 1 & 3	Pass 1 & 3	Pass 1 & 3	Pass 1 & 3	Pass 1 & 3
	A.M.	A.M.	P.M.	P.M.	P.M.	P.M.	P.M.
Peterhead depart	6·15	9·25	12 20	3·0	Fridays and Saturdays only.	5·20	7·5
Inverugie	6·22	9·30	12·24	3·4		5·25	7·9
New Seat	6·26	9·34	12·28	3·8		5·29	7·13
Longside	6·33	9·41	12·35	3·15		5·36	7·20
Old Deer and Mintlaw ...	6·43	9·51	12·45	3·24		5·46	7·30
New Maud Junction arrive (Formerly Brucklay.)	6·54	10·3	12·56	3·35		5·57	7·45
Fraserburgh depart ...	6·0	9·15	12·0	...		5·5	Fridays and Saturdays only.
Rathen	6·8	9·23	12·8	...		5·13	
Lonmay	6·15	9·30	12·16	...		5·20	
Mormond	6·24	9·38	12 22	...		5·27	
Strichen	6·32	9·55	12·29	...		5·34	
Brucklay	6·44	9·56	12·31	...		5·46	
New Maud Junction ar.	6·53	10·3	12·50	...		5·55	
New Maud Junction dep.	7·0	10·5	12·58	...	...	6·0	
Auchnagatt	7·12	10·16	1·9	...	...	6·12	
Arnage	7·24	10·27	1·20	...	...	6·24	
Ellon	7·35	10·38	1·32	...	4·25	6·35	
Esslemont	7·40	10·43	1·37	...	4·30	6·40	
Logierieve	7·45	10·49	1·42	...	...	6·45	
Udny	7·50	10·53	1·48	...	4·40	6·55	
Newmachar	8 0	11·4	2·0	...	4·49	7·6	
Parkhill	8·15	11·15	2·14	...	5·0	7·17	
Dyce Junction arrive ...	8·20	11·19	2·20	...	5·4	7·21	
Dyce Junction depart ...	8·24	11·20	2·21	...	5·5	7·24	...
Buxburn	8·30	11·25	2·28	...	5·11	7·30	...
Woodside	8 36	11·29	2·32	...	...	7·34	...
Kittybrewster	8·48	11·34	2·40	...	5·21	7·40	...
Aberdeen arrive	8·58	11·40	2·50	...	5·30	7·50	...

Return Tickets at One and a Half Ordinary Fares daily, available to return on day of issue.
Return Tickets on SATURDAYS, at One Ordinary Fare, available to return on day of issue, or on MONDAY following.

CHEAP FARES FOR FISHERWOMEN.

Third Class Tickets at One Ordinary Fare issued to Fisherwomen at Fraserburgh, Rathen, Lonmay, and Peterhead, to Aberdeen or any intermediate Station, available to return on day of issue or day following. One Creel Load of Fish allowed to each free of charge, and any additional Package charged Goods' Rates.

☞ Passengers Booked Through from Peterhead and Fraserburgh to Edinburgh, Glasgow, London, &c.

CHEAP FARE TO EDINBURGH.

On THURSDAYS, Passengers are Booked Third Class from Fraserburgh by 12 0 P.M. Train, and from Peterhead by 12·20 P.M. Train to Edinburgh at 13s. 6d.

GOODS TRAFFIC.

Information as to Rates, Delivery of Goods, &c., &c., will be obtained on application to the TRAFFIC MANAGER, Waterloo Station, Aberdeen, the AGENTS at the respective Stations, or Messrs MUTTER, HOWEY, & Co., Agents for the Company at Fraserburgh, Peterhead, Aberdeen, &c.

For further particulars, Conditions on which Tickets are issued, &c., &c., see the Company's Time Tables.

By order,

ROBERT MILNE, Gen. Manager.

Company's Office, Waterloo Station, Aberdeen, 20th April 1865.

(Above) The first timetable to show the whole line, as published in the local newspapers.

(Below and right) Sample tickets from the collection of Ross Kerby.

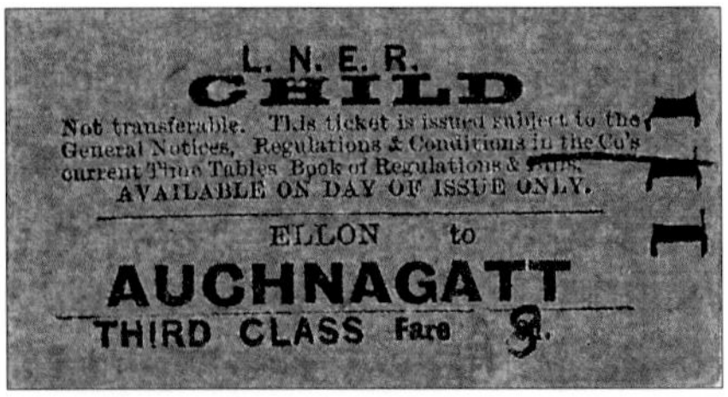

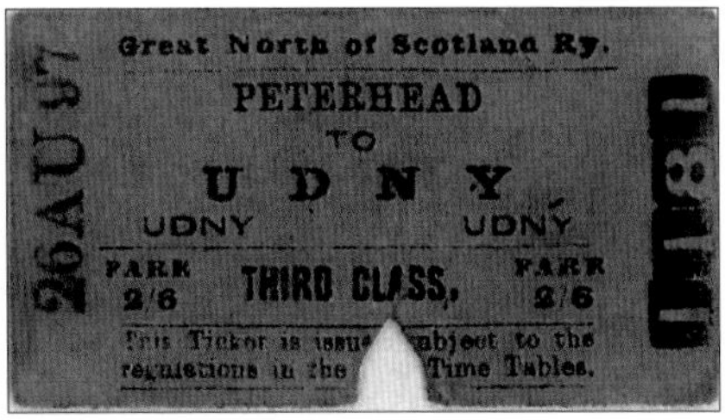

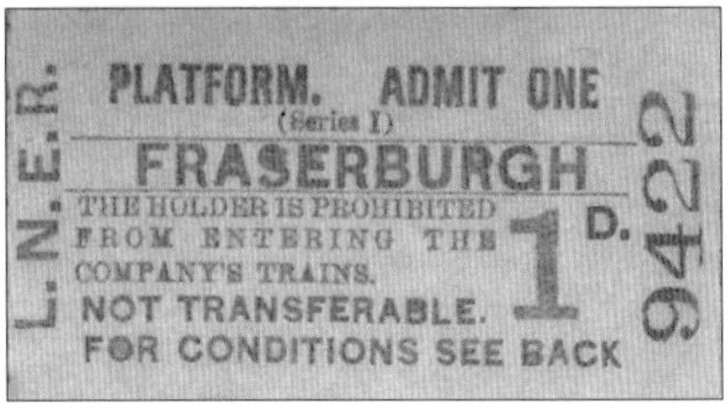

The Formartine & Buchan Railway

Railways came to Aberdeenshire in the 1850s and 1860s. Following the opening of the first section of the Great North of Scotland Railway from Aberdeen to Huntly in 1854, branches were promoted in all directions. Naturally, the important towns of Peterhead and Fraserburgh featured in these proposals. In fact, such was their significance that two rival schemes were proposed, one starting at Dyce and following an inland route and the other a coastal route from Aberdeen. This had the result of delaying the building of the line.

The Formartine & Buchan Railway, from Dyce, was finally authorised in 1858 and opened in stages, reaching Mintlaw in 1861, Peterhead in 1862 and Fraserburgh in 1865. By comparison, lines to Banff, Macduff and Alford were all opened before any part of the Buchan line. Even Speyside was rail connected before Fraserburgh. Although constructed by a separate company, the Buchan line was operated from the start by the Great North of Scotland Railway and became part of it in 1866.

Two extension were constructed. In 1897, a branch was opened from Ellon to Cruden Bay and Boddam. Its terminus was just a few miles south of Peterhead and if it had been extended there the distance to Peterhead would have been significantly shortened. The GNSR built a luxurious new hotel at Cruden Bay along with a golf course. The golf course is still in use, but the hotel was never very successful commercially and only in use during the summer season. It was demolished after the Second World War. From Fraserburgh, a line was opened in 1903 to the fishing village of St Combs. This was popular for journeys in to Fraserburgh.

The coming of the railway had a dramatic impact on life in Buchan. Before then, coaches provided a limited service. In 1850, the *Earl of Errol* ran from Aberdeen to Peterhead in five hours; it could accommodate four passengers inside and eight outside at fares to Peterhead of 10/- inside and 5/- outside. The *Banks of Ythan* ran twice a week to Strichen and twice a week to Old Deer.

Once the railway opened, Aberdeen became a day trip away. Mails were delivered in the morning, although an early complaint was that the timing of the mail trains to and from Peterhead

Staff at Lonmay in the 1920s. Parcels and other small items, often in wicker baskets such as these, were a staple part of railway traffic until the 1960s.
(GNSRA Collection)

When William Ferguson's Guide to the Great North of Scotland Railway was published in 1881, several sketches were prepared to illustrate it. But it was found that they were too costly to be used so they were published separately. This illustration of Inverugie Castle was among them.

Helioᵍʳˢ et Imp A Durand Paris

only allowed half an hour for a letter to be answered the same day. The timetable for 1865, illustrated on page 6, shows the service for the first few years. The journey time to Peterhead was now half that by coach, although it still took 2½ hours for 40 miles.

Trains in those days consisted of four-wheeled carriages with wooden seats in third class. First class passengers had padded seats and more room. An early comment was that the trains ran very smoothly. That must have been compared with road coaches; early trains were by no means smooth when compared with train travel today.

The railway played an important part in the development of the fishing industry. Steam powered vessels came into use in the 1880s and these required larger ports, so both Fraserburgh and Peterhead grew in importance. Refrigerated transport followed, ensuring that fresh fish got to distant markets in Scotland and England. Fast trains were introduced from Aberdeen to take the fish south. Herring shoals moved around the coast each year, followed by many Buchan 'fisher lassies' who travelled each year to east coast fishing ports as far south as Great Yarmouth to process the catches.

Agriculture benefitted greatly from the coming of the railways. Fertiliser, in the form of lime or manure, was brought in to improve crop yields, while produce was despatched. Aberdeen Angus cattle proved popular and this helped the development of the auction mart at Maud, which relied on the railway to take the cattle south.

The line was very busy in the Victorian and Edwardian periods. Traffic increased during the First World War as coastal shipping was stopped and it was still significant in the 1920s, but then road competition developed. Passengers deserted to the more frequent and often cheaper bus services. Peterhead in particular suffered due to the length of the route via Maud. The last passenger train to Boddam ran in 1932, but freight and parcels traffic continued.

During the 1950s and early 1960s, the increasing cost of operating the line was not matched by an increase in revenue. By 1961, steam trains had been replaced by diesels. Even so, this was not enough to save the passenger service on the line and it was included in the Beeching Report. The last trains to St Combs and Peterhead ran in May 1965, followed by the end of services to Fraserburgh in October that year.

Freight trains continued for a few years more. The last traffic to Peterhead was for Crosse & Blackwell but when that switched to road in 1970, the line from Maud closed. Fraserburgh continued to handle a range of traffic throughout the 1970s. Maud received pipes for the then booming north sea oil and gas industry for onward transport by road to Peterhead. But little maintenance was undertaken on the track. In 1979, the significant expenditure needed could not be justified, so the line closed completely. The trackbed was acquired by Grampian Regional Council as the basis for the Formartine and Buchan Way. Reopening the line has been mentioned on many occasions, particularly on the section to Ellon. That is always a possibility.

Along the line, most of the stations have survived. Although small, the buildings constructed in the 1860s are solid and have been expanded to form modern homes. The larger buildings at Peterhead and Fraserburgh have been completely demolished and other uses found for the sites. Maud was converted for commercial use. Mintlaw was treated in the same way but a subsequent fire left it derelict. You can spot several of these buildings along the line but please respect the privacy of the occupants.

The history of the line is comprehensively described in *Railways of Buchan*, published by the Great North of Scotland Railway Association.

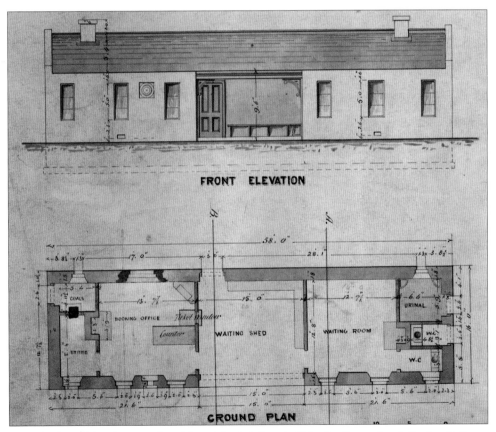

Several coloured drawings survive of the original stations built for the Formartine & Buchan Railway. This is Brucklay. Later in the 19th century, the open centre section facing the platform was enclosed behind a wooden screen to provide more protection for waiting passengers.   *(GNSR Association)*

The Formartine and Buchan Way forms a superb linear habitat for wildlife. Relatively free from disturbance the varied flora provides food and shelter for many insects, birds and mammals. Stations such as Arnage (above) are gradually reverting back to nature as wildflowers spread over the platform. In early summer many sheltered sections of the Line, as at Pitfour (below), are lush with greenery and fragrant with hawthorn blossom.

Wildlife Along The Way

Work to develop the Formartine and Buchan Way started in 1979, largely driven by the Buchan Countryside Group with support and cooperation from Grampian Regional Council (since superseded by Aberdeen City and Aberdeenshire Councils). This ambitious project to create a 54 mile long wildlife corridor and continuous footpath and cycleway stretching from Dyce to Fraserburgh and Peterhead benefitted from funding from bodies including Scottish Natural Heritage and the European Agricultural Guidance and Guarantee Fund. Although the then Scottish Minister for Transport and the Environment, Sarah Boyack MSP, conducted an initial opening ceremony near the Don viaduct on 12 June 2000, prolonged negotiations with landowners and other factors delayed the final completion of the route until 2013.

Unlike the prime farmland through which it passes, the Line is relatively free from disturbance and the use of agrichemicals and so forms an important linear habitat for wildlife.

Dog roses

The Line's varied flora – flowers, bushes and trees – provides a valuable source of food and shelter for birds and mammals. The vegetation marks the changing seasons and gives each section its own character, from the barren, windswept miles of the north to the sheltered stretch through the great estates of Aden and Pitfour in the 'Garden of Buchan' and the gentle rolling countryside of the Ebrie valley. . Many sections of the permanent way appear to be hedged by almost constantly flowering yellow gorse, or by fragrant Dog Roses, both white and pink forms, which later in the year produce scarlet hips. Some stations, notably Arnage and Rathen, seem to be reverting to the wild. The platform edges at Arnage are engulfed in a tangle of Lesser Periwinkle and Honeysuckle whilst the platform itself is being invaded by celandines, primroses, saplings and daffodils gradually encroaching from the nearby policies of Arnage Castle.

The seasons are marked by the emergence of differing species of lineside flora. Early in the year, along with the first snowdrops

Celandines

the strange, cauliflower like inflorescences of butterbur appear in damp places such as the banks of the Ugie by Deer Abbey and of the Ebrie at Mill of Elrick. The butterbur flowers appear long before their huge rhubarb like leaves - traditionally used to wrap butter. Several sections of the Line, notably the approaches to Longside from the west and around Auchnagatt, are lined with

Snowdrops

Willow catkins

willows, their silky catkins providing early sustenance for bees. The small bright yellow stars of lesser celandine open on sunny spring days in ditches and moist places. The knobbly tuberous root of this plant is a traditional herbal remedy for haemorrhoids hence the common name of 'Pilewort'. The larger egg yolk yellow flowers of marsh marigolds appear in similar damp locations a little later in the spring. Each April, below the viaduct over the Ugie in Strichen, a great drift of the delicate

Marsh marigolds

nodding white wood anemone appears in the damp grass. There is an unexpectedly beautiful meadow opposite the industrial sites close to the southern end of the Line which in May is studded with pale mauve lady's smock and bright yellow field buttercups interspersed with the occasional mauve spike of wild orchids.

By midsummer the frothy leaves and creamy white flowers of sweet cicely, easily distinguished from similar related plants by their distinctive aniseed smell, adorn damper sections. The shade under bridges provides conditions for the tiny starry pink flowers of pink purslane and in the shade of trees by Aden Country Park the strange, ghostly flowers of enchanter's nightshade, uncommon in the north of Scotland, flourish. The drier sections of embankment south of Newmachar are studded with the white moons of ox-eye daisy, mingling with the vivid russet of orange hawkweed, whimsically also known as fox and cubs.

Wood anemones

In late summer mile after mile of the Line is flanked by the bright purplish-rose spikes of rosebay willow. Now an invasive and widespread weed, rosebay was considered a rare and desirable garden plant until the mid-eighteenth century when it began to appear occasionally in the wild. It thrives in newly disturbed ground particularly where burning has occurred, hence the plant's alternative name of 'fireweed'. However, rosebay has spread rapidly during the last hundred and fifty years or so; the disturbance of the ground as the railway was being constructed, followed by occasional fires started by sparks from steam locomotives, provided ideal conditions for the plant which, once established, throve and colonised miles of embankments. On warm autumn days the gorse and broom catapult seeds from pea-like pods, often with sharp explosive sound, as the multitudinous seed heads of the rosebay willow herb drift on silky threads over the Line.

Not all lineside flora can be considered as truly wild; here and there garden escapees or deliberate plantings

Butterbur

have colonised the embankments and gladden the passing walker's heart. Close to the Aden Estate, sections of the embankment have been densely and pungently colonised by few flowered leek, an invasive escapee. In April and May the delicate drooping white flowers and strap like leaves of this native of the Caucasus and Iran cover the lineside under and around the bridge carrying the Fetterangus to Old Deer road over the Line to the dense exclusion of other plants. An arresting patch of scarlet oriental poppies blooms annually in early summer on the bank where the Line crosses the B9093 just east of Strichen and close to where the far humbler tricoloured heartsease pansies flower in the sandy embankment. At Atherb, close to Brucklay station, a vast spread of the elegant, arching stems of Solomon's seal, hung with pale bell shaped flowers, enjoys the shade of beech trees. Fuchsia and buddleia, the latter a magnet for butterflies, are occasionally naturalised along the embankments and provide splashes of colour in late summer. There are occasional fruit trees, such as

Few flowered leek

apples and pears, which have probably grown from cores long ago jettisoned by snacking train passengers.

The vegetation along the permanent way abounds with insects, birds and usually shy

Solomon's seal

mammals. Bird life changes throughout the season but there are always small busy flocks of finches and tits flitting from resting point to resting point along the telegraph wires. Flocks of chaffinches and goldfinches, the latter sporting cheerful sealing wax red masks round their beaks, feed on seed heads; thistles are an especial favourite. In summer they are joined by swallows and martins swooping low over the fields in graceful arcs as they hunt flying insects or scoop up a beak full of mud for nest building. At Mill of Elrick an osprey occasionally snatches fish from the ponds. The autumn brings the great honking skeins of pink footed geese winging across the sky as they commute between their evening roosts (65,000 at Strathbeg alone) and the stubble fields where they graze during the day. Lovely silver arrows of whooper swans, longer necked and flying lower than the geese, have a distinctive trumpeting call. Wet fields, prone to flooding, attract herons, curlews and the occasional clowning flock of lapwings with their distinctive tumbling flight. Flocks of smart black and white oystercatchers are easily distinguished by their bright beaks and legs probing winter fields for insects with their bright orange bills. Increasingly frequently buzzards may be seen soaring high above woodlands.

Mammals are more elusive – there can hardly be a mile of the Line which is not home to rabbits burrowing into the embankment but there are less frequently seen creatures such as hedgehogs snuffling about at dusk hunting slugs and snails or the shy roe deer, agile and noiseless. There are sudden brief glimpses of sinuous, sleek stoats, chestnut brown in summer, but more often seen in a white winter coat – conspicuous when there is no snow – streaking across the Line. They, like foxes, hunt the smaller mammals – mice, voles and rabbits which populate the bushes and embankments. Brucklay Station is named for the badgers (brocks) which, historically, lived in the vicinity. Close to the Line between Deer Abbey and Aden there is a large, well established badger sett – its inhabitants are almost exclusively nocturnal.

These two views of Fraserburgh from similar positions were taken over fifty years apart. The spires of Dalrymple Hall and Fraserburgh South Parish Church link the two. The station and extensive sidings to the right have all been swept away, although the engine shed, which is behind the steam locomotive to the left of the station, still stands and can be found behind the building in the centre of the lower photograph.   *(Above, Arthur Bower, GNSRA)*

Walking the Line : Fraserburgh to Maud

The actual route of the railway line out of Fraserburgh is now followed by Harbour Road. The Ordnance Survey Explorer map sheet 427 indicates the route of the Formartine and Buchan Way as leading up Station Brae turning left onto Seaforth Street, passing the South Church, then following the path to the right of the Leisure Centre and skirting the edge of the Links to Links Road before dropping down to Harbour Road and along the Esplanade to where the trackbed is picked up behind the children's play area.

Fraserburgh Railway Station (NJ 999 667): Fraserburgh railway station, suitably close to the harbour on what in 1932 became Station Brae, was partially built on the site of former boilyards, a relic of the brief period of Greenland whale and seal fishing by Fraserburgh boats. This venture began in the 1850s and lasted for around a decade, the handful of boats involved meeting with very little success. It was abandoned by the early 1860s. When the station opened in 1865 it comprised a single platform and a locomotive shed. This original shed, having survived a fire in March 2002, still stands surrounded by a fish yard on Harbour Road below the South Church.

The opening of Fraserburgh Station was an occasion of great pomp and ceremony, attended by the great and good of Fraserburgh, the surrounding villages and the dignitaries of the railway company. On Saturday 22 April, two days before the railway opened to fare paying passengers, a special train brought the directors of the company to Fraserburgh to attend a grand celebratory dinner for 200 held in the Harbour Commissioners Hall. Unfortunately, the train arrived 10 minutes early so that the formal reception was cancelled and the local Volunteers were too late to line the streets for the parade of dignitaries through the town. However a feu-de-joie was fired by the battery at the Castle Park and a display of rockets took place in the evening as the visiting dignitaries left the town. On the following Monday, a local holiday, vast numbers of people took advantage of the special excursion trains to have their first experience of railway travel.

In 1903 the station was completely redesigned and rebuilt to accommodate the St Combs Line. The enlarged station boasted a rather grand booking hall and two island platforms with

The engine shed at Fraserburgh is all that remains of the station.

The baronial tower of Dalrymple Hall, positioned on Station Brae opposite the entrance to Fraserburgh Station, would have given passengers arriving in the town the impression of a confident prosperous community.

an elaborate canopy; the St Combs Line used the platform on the east side. The volume of water used by the railway engines made such huge demands on the town's water supply that water had to be rationed in summer. To overcome this the railway piped water from springs at Futret Den, Percyhorner, and sold some of the water back to the town.

The goods yard at the station was adjacent to the fish market and harbour so fish could easily be loaded for transport south. Extensive sidings accommodated the wagons needed for this traffic. During the herring boom of the 1890s so many wagons were required that sidings at Rathen and Lonmay in addition to Fraserburgh were used to store them. The catch was sped south on the 'Fish Specials' which took precedence over passenger trains. Fish was also imported to Fraserburgh by train from Mallaig for processing at the town's fish factories. In the early autumn special trains, organised by the fish curing firm by whom they were employed, carried the 'gutting quines' and all their goods and chattels to East Anglian ports where they gutted and packed the herring.

Following the closure of the Fraserburgh line to passengers from 4 October 1965 and to freight from 8 October 1979, the grandeur of the station ensured that it had status as a listed building until it was completely gutted by fire in 1982, still empty and awaiting a new use.

Dalrymple Hall (NJ 998 667): The splendidly baronial Dalrymple Hall was built in 1881 directly opposite what would have been the main entrance to the station: its imposing design befits a period of growth and civic pride in the Broch. The hall and the street behind it were named after the Dalrymple family, prominent Fraserburgh shipbuilders who donated the land on which it was built. This ambitious building, with its five storey baronial tower topped by a weather vane in the form of a drifter, originally housed a cafe, dining room, newsroom, public hall, public baths and, once a month, the sheriff court. For many years it was the venue for the most prestigious events in the Fraserburgh social calendar. The building is now an arts centre. The 'Silver Beetles', later to become 'The Beatles', performed here on 23 May 1960 during their Scottish tour; they were not well received.

Former Station Hotel (NJ 997 667): illustrated above right.

The former station hotel at Fraserburgh. The pediment over the window indicates that the building was hastily converted from two houses to meet the need for accommodation once the railway arrived.

Fraserburgh West Parish Church (NJ 994 667): Fraserburgh West Parish Church was built in 1876 and now stands on a traffic island, known locally as The Hexagon, formed by the junction of several of the main Victorian streets of the town. The church's elegant steeple forms a prominent landmark on the Fraserburgh skyline.

The church was built during the Victorian expansion of Fraserburgh for those parishioners of the original Old Parish Church who had moved out to the new, fashionable and prosperous district *'among the green fields high on a slope on the edge of the town'*. (Cranna)

Fraserburgh South Church (NJ 998 667): Fraserburgh South Church occupies the site of the eighteenth century parish school on Seaforth Street and overlooks Fraserburgh Leisure Centre, Bellslea football ground and the Links – almost directly above the old station. Originally the South United Free Church, it was built between 1878 and 1880 in a towering Germanic Gothic style. It contains the Moses Stone, depicting Moses receiving the Ten Commandments and dated 1613; the stone is thought to be the only relic of the short lived Fraserburgh University.

Fraserburgh University had a vague and troubled history; there is disagreement and conjecture as to its exact location, and if it ever actually enrolled students. All that is certain is that the University was located at the west side of Fraserburgh, towards Broadsea probably in the vicinity of the Denmark Street area and what, since 1870, has been known as College Bounds. This supposition is largely based on the discovery in that area of vaulted cellars and sculptured stones, including the Moses Stone.

The Moses Stone is widely thought to have been designed either as an altar stone or to be placed above the main entrance to the University buildings. The date on the stone, 1613, was the date of Sir Alexander Fraser of Philorth's contract with the feuars of the Broch which established the town council and merchant guild and granted rights regarding the holding of markets and annual fairs.

In 1787 the Moses Stone was mounted in the wall above the door of the old parish school on the Links. When the South Kirk was built on the site the stone was inserted in the south wall of the kirk. In 1969 it was moved inside to prevent further damage by the elements.

Fraserburgh University was founded by charter in 1592 and financed largely by Sir Alexander Fraser of Philorth as part of his attempt to assist the growth of the town. This charter also changed 'Faithlie' the older name for the town, to Fraserburgh. Sir Alexander's efforts

The curve of the railway as it sweeps along Fraserburgh Bay was the inspiration for the clean lines of the Walking Way sculpture on the Links – designed to connect the Leisure Centre car park with the seafront.

to improve Fraserburgh incurred huge debts, forcing him to sell part of his estate which in turn reduced the income for the university. The first and probably only principal was Charles Ferme, graduate of Edinburgh University and Presbyterian minister of the Parish Church of Philorth (Fraserburgh). Ferme arrived in Fraserburgh in 1598 but was soon imprisoned for his opposition to Episcopacy. He subsequently returned to Fraserburgh where he died in 1617 and was buried at Kirkton. It is generally thought that the University did not survive Ferme's imprisonment and Lord Saltoun's reduced fortunes, along with the growth of its rival, Marischal College in Aberdeen, founded by the Earl Marischal, Keith of Inverugie, in 1593. The University building was probably used to house students and staff of King's College during an outbreak of plague in Aberdeen in 1647-1648.

The Links (NJ 998 664): The Links were granted to the townspeople of Fraserburgh as common grazing by Sir Alexander Fraser in the 1613 charter. Originally stretching from Bellslea to the Cairnbulg Road they have been used, over the centuries, for a variety of purposes: religious, industrial, recreational, military and educational. Until the early twentieth century, it was not unusual for people to keep cows and horses in yards attached to their property and to turn them out to graze on the Links daily, walking the cows home through the streets to be milked.

In 1803 a rope and sail works, owned by Alexander Malcolm, was established on the Links close to Bellslea Park and the present South Church. It flourished for about half a century, employing a considerable number of men. The works met its demise when the decline in big sailing ships coincided with the growth of larger, more mechanised rope works in the south which produced cheaper goods.

Golf was played on the Links from around 1770 until 1891, by which time the Links had become so busy that golf balls were a danger to pedestrians. The players used a feather filled ball and 'holes' consisting of granite cups sunk permanently into the grass.

At various times, including during the Napoleonic Wars, when local companies of Volunteers defended Fraserburgh against the threat of invasion the Links has been used as a drill and parade ground by the military.

Vast crowds of excited people from Fraserburgh and the surrounding villages congregated on the Links on 22 April 1865 when the first train steamed in to Fraserburgh Station. This was the first time that most of the crowd had seen a steam locomotive and many were too apprehensive about the possibility of '*the train taking it into its head to try some gymnastics on the Links*' (Cranna) to stand too close to the railway line. Evidently it was a common misconception that railway accidents occurred so frequently that it would be foolhardy to approach too closely.

In August 1904 the Links became the scene of an extraordinary spectacle when, watched by an estimated audience of 19,000, Buffalo Bill (Colonel Wild Bill Codey) and his Indian Braves performed an extraordinary extravaganza involving 500 horses and over 800 people, including Annie Oakley. The company arrived in Fraserburgh in three special trains consisting of 49 wagons specially adapted to carry the livestock, which included elephants, the set and performers.

The first aeroplane to be seen in Fraserburgh landed on the Links during the summer of 1913. Large crowds of astonished Brochers flocked to see the biplane piloted by Captain Dawes of the Naval Wing of the Royal Flying Corps. The plane was almost certainly heading for the Cromarty Firth where a suitable site for a base was being sought.

Since 2007 the railway has been celebrated by 'The Walking Way', a prominent sculpture of steel girders and oak beams, on the seaward side of the Links. Designed by sculptural artist Jane Kelly, it was inspired by the railway which ran directly below the installation.

The Saltoun Place Fountain and the Burgh School (NJ 997 665): The gloriously ornate iron dome surmounted by a key carrying ostrich which sticks up above the dyke on the landward side of the Links forms the pinnacle of the Saltoun Place Fountain. The fountain was erected in 1904 and prior to 1923 stood on the current site of the War Memorial at the junction of Strichen Road and Saltoun Place. The prefabricated cast-iron fountain was produced by Walter MacFarlane and Co., Saracen Foundry, Glasgow and was customised for Fraserburgh by topping the canopy with an ostrich holding the key to the burgh. This bird, derived from the ostrich which appears holding a horseshoe in the Saltoun coat of arms, is incorporated in the former burgh coat of arms which also appear on the fountain. A plaque on the pavement by the fountain commemorates Charles Alfred Jarvis, VC, who is described in the section on the Admiralty Buildings below.

The Saltoun Fountain with the former Burgh School in the background on the right.

The low building to the north of the fountain was the burgh school between 1838 and 1882 when the pupils moved to the newly opened Central School. Astonishingly given the small size of the building, it could cater for up to 200 pupils and was known locally as Mr Woodman's School, after the headmaster who served there for an extraordinary 43 years. Following the closure of the school the building has had various uses including a businessmen's club and during the Second World War an ARP first aid clinic, later becoming a doctors' surgery and finally a pre-school nursery.

Thomas Blake Glover, who is widely regarded as being responsible for the development and industrialisation of modern Japan, began his education at the parish school. Glover, the son of a coastguard, was born on 6 June 1838 at 15 Commerce Street (the house was destroyed during an air raid in World War 2) and attended the parish school before the family moved to Aberdeen. By 1859 Thomas had become a merchant in Nagasaki, at first largely trading in tea. During the Japanese Civil War Glover was able to utilise his expertise in commerce to amass a vast fortune by trading in arms and ships. In 1908 his huge contribution to Japanese

Admiralty Buildings, the former coastguard houses, which was the birthplace of Charles Jarvis VC.

industrialisation and development was recognised when he became the first non-Japanese to be awarded the Order of the Rising Sun, one of the highest Japanese honours. There is a theory, based on the tenuous evidence that in some pictures Glover's Japanese wife is seen wearing a kimono decorated with butterflies, that Puccini's opera Madam Butterfly is based upon the life of Glover.

Admiralty Buildings (NJ 997 664): More familiar locally as 'The Coastguard Houses' this terrace, backing on to the Links, was built in 1869 by the Admiralty for use as a coastguard station. The buildings included a house for the station officer and six cottages for his staff and had unobstructed views of the sea.

Charles Alfred Jarvis, one of the first soldiers to be awarded a Victoria Cross in World War 1 was born here in 1881, shortly before his coastguard father was transferred to Rattray. Lance-Cpl Jarvis earned the VC for his bravery in blowing up the Bridge of Jemappes on 23 August 1914, during the retreat from Mons. Jarvis Court sheltered housing and day care centre in Fraserburgh is named in his honour.

Fraserburgh Bay (NK 020 640): The 18th century attempt to develop Fraserburgh as a spa town with mineral springs, pump rooms and tidal seawater baths (cut out of the rock by Kinnaird Castle) was less successful than the later development of the burgh as a seaside resort.

Between 1912 and 1914 excavation of the harbour produced material which was used to start building the beach promenade. Over the years the esplanade has boasted a cafe, bathing pavilion, children's playground, miniature railway, sealife centre and caravan park. A post World War 2 tourist guide to Fraserburgh confidently boasts that the beach '*becomes more popular every year, which is but natural as it only needs to be known to become famous as a holiday playground. Every season something more is added to the facilities provided for visitors, but the chief attractions of Fraserburgh Bay will always be its golden sands, its blue waters and crested waves, and the sunshine of which Fraserburgh enjoys more than the average supply*'.

The sea air and 3 miles of magnificent beach brought tourists to the burgh in the immediate post war years but visitors declined following the closure of the railway and the availability of package holidays to less bracing destinations. The caravan park still attracts many visitors and there is excellent surf.

The Golden Horn (NK 003 668): The lighthouse standing 22 metres above high water mark at the end of the pier is sometimes known as the Golden Horn. It perhaps gets its name from the lucky gold sovereign said to have been embedded in the base of the tower when it was built around 1882. The first stage of the pier was completed during the Crimean War and was named to commemorate the Battle of Balaclava. The extension to the Pier was one of the first major marine structures in Scotland to be built entirely of concrete.

Prior to the extending of the Balaclava Pier and the building of a breakwater, entering the harbour during rough seas was extremely perilous. The laying of the foundation stone of the breakwater by Lord Saltoun on 23 October 1875 was an occasion of great pageantry. As part of the celebratory parade Lord Saltoun was ceremoniously seated in a Broadsea yawl mounted on a specially built under-carriage and pulled from the North Lodge at Philorth to the pier by 100 appreciative Broadsea fishermen.

Kinnaird Head Lighthouse (NJ 998 676): The massive white tower of Kinnaird Head Castle, surmounted by the lighthouse, is a conspicuous landmark on the approach to the Broch along the Line. The castle was built by the Frasers of Philorth around 1570 and was sold to the Trustees of the Northern Lighthouse Board in 1787. The lighthouse has the dual distinctions of being the first to be built on mainland Scotland and of being the only lighthouse to be positioned on top of a 16th century castle. The original whale oil light had a range of 12 miles, making it the most powerful beam of the time. Unfortunately, the lighthouse structure weighed so much that it caused damage to the castle. In 1824 Lighthouse Board engineer, Robert Stevenson, grandfather of Robert Louis Stevenson, redesigned the lighthouse to be less heavy. On 20 March 1929 Kinnaird became the first British location to warn ships by radio beacon; it was decommissioned in 1991 and now houses the Museum of Scottish Lighthouses.

Kinnaird Head gets its name from the Gaelic *'cinn na h'airde'*, meaning *'the headland at the point of land'*, which aptly fits the promontory location. The headland overlooks the harbour and it is thought possible that even before the building of the first official lighthouse the castle keep may have had a beacon to guide vessels towards the safety of the harbour or round the coast. There are superb views of the coastline from the top of the lighthouse where there was an aircraft spotting post during the Second World War.

Nobel Prize winning Italian physicist, Guglielmo Marconi, inventor of wireless telegraphy, conducted Scotland's earliest radio experiments in Fraserburgh in 1904 when he successfully transmitted a signal from a shack on Broadsea Farm, close to present day Marconi Road, to Poldhu in Cornwall. This was part of his project to link transmitters in Norway, Iceland and Poldhu so that radio communication with fishing boats in the North Sea would be possible. There is a replica of Marconi's shack in Fraserburgh Heritage Centre which is adjacent to the Museum of Scottish Lighthouses.

'The Golden Horn' lighthouse.

Fraserburgh Old Parish Church (NJ 998 671): The present church dates from 1803, when it replaced an earlier parish church, and is the oldest place of worship still in use in Fraserburgh. The stubby spire was intended to be taller but money ran out before it was completed. Even so it was lofty enough to be seen from miles around and was described by Cranna as '*The distinguished landmark which guided the weary and storm tossed mariner into a safe channel for taking Fraserburgh Harbour...Until other buildings dwarfed the church it was always given in Mariner's Guide Books and tide tables as a mark to steer for from a given point of the compass when running for Fraserburgh Harbour*'.

Fraserburgh Townhouse (NJ 998 671): Fraserburgh townhouse, surmounted by a rotunda and almost adjacent to the Old Parish Church, was built between 1853 and 1855 to replace the old Tolbooth. The rotunda surmounts the round entrance tower which houses a statue of 'The Waterloo Saltoun', Alexander 16th Lord Saltoun, who distinguished himself in many military campaigns including Waterloo.

The townhouse contained the police station, courtroom and town hall above a market. During the summer of 1874, at the height of the herring season, the doors and windows of the building were damaged by a riotous hoard of around 2000 inebriated west coast fishermen. As the Highlanders poured out of public houses at closing time they became increasingly disorderly, attacking the town house where they thought that their ring leader had been imprisoned. Alarmed locals began to retaliate. It was only with the arrival by train from Aberdeen of a detachment of Gordon Highlanders that the riot was quelled.

Fraserburgh Academy (NJ 991 664): The shallow, trapezium shaped, reddish roof is part of Fraserburgh Academy situated in Dennyduff Road. The roof is part of the building constructed in 1962, opposite an earlier building, now the art department, which was opened in 1909.

One of the most famous former pupils of the academy was William Elphinstone Gibb, better known as 60s fashion designer, Bill Gibb. Gibb's flair for using historical and natural motifs in fantastical, exotic designs in a mixture of fabrics matched the mood of 1960s London and he was rapidly acknowledged as a cutting edge designer. His clothes, incorporating his embroidered bee trademark, were worn by stars including Bianca Jagger and Twiggy. Some of his most successful designs were for intricate knitwear, produced in collaboration with Kaffe Fassett. Bill Gibb died of cancer in 1988. Examples of his work are on display in Fraserburgh Heritage Centre.

Cairnbulg Briggs (NK 037 660): The beacon which marks the treacherous rocks at Cairnbulg Briggs is at the east end of Fraserburgh Bay beyond the mouth of the Water of Philorth. Despite the white warning light flashed every 10 seconds by the beacon during the hours of darkness, many vessels have come to grief on the Briggs. The wreck of the Banff registered *Sovereign*, which went aground on 18 December 2005 and is visible about 50 metres off shore, featured on the publicity poster for the 2012 film 'Life of Pi'.

Consolidated Pneumatic Tool Company Factory (NJ 999 659): The grim row of grey, industrial buildings on the landward side of the Line was the former Consolidated Pneumatic Tool Company factory which was associated with Fraserburgh for over eight decades, ceasing production at the end of 1987. The American company began making pneumatic drills in the town around 1903 before diversifying production to include other pneumatic tools and compressors. The pneumatic hammers used on the Sydney Harbour Bridge were made here. In 1914 CPT began to make the portable power tools used by munitions manufacturers, becoming a major supplier of the British arms industry. In World War 2 CPT produced fuel pumps and booster controls for the Rolls Royce Merlin engines used in Spitfires. Fraserburgh became an important centre for the manufacture of munitions employing a workforce of almost 2,500, including over 1000 women. Unfortunately, the vast factory made an easy target for enemy planes approaching over the North Sea from Norway and became one of the reasons that Fraserburgh suffered such a disproportionate number of air raids that the area became known as 'Hellfire Corner'.

The CPT building was designed by an American architect Louis Christian Mullgardt, who incorporated an almost unique design feature, a 'saw toothed roof' set into pitched gables designed to maximise natural light levels in the workshop below. This roof, visible from Kessock Road, is thought to be the only surviving example and was granted Category C Listed Building status in December 2012.

Kirkton Pillbox (NK 001 657): The remains of a strategically placed Second World War pillbox can be seen to the west of the Line in the field opposite the main gates of the graveyard. This example is a type 24 pillbox with embrasures designed to accommodate light machine guns and was one of several defences put in place to reduce the risk of an enemy landing. The remains of further pillboxes are still partially buried on the bents and beach.

St Combs Light Railway (NK 004 654): Affectionately known as the 'Belger Trainie', the St Combs Light Railway opened on 1 July 1903 and served the fishing communities of Cairnbulg and St Combs. The Light Railway Act of 1896 was a government attempt to boost the rural economy and to support communities which were isolated from the main rail network by promoting the construction of cheaper railways. Axle loads were limited to 8 tons and speed to 25 mph. The 5 mile journey took 17 minutes. Sections of the line were unfenced so the trains were fitted with cow catchers.

    The St Combs Line must have been one of the earliest 'pay trains' in Scotland as from March 1918 guards issued tickets to passengers boarding the train at Kirkton Bridge and Philorth Bridge Halt. This was extended in November 1960 when the stations at Cairnbulg and St Combs were unstaffed, only the ticket office at Fraserburgh remaining open. Complete closure of the line followed in May 1965.

Kirkton Burial ground (NK 001 658): Fraserburgh (Fraser's burgh) developed from the medieval settlement of Faithlie largely due to the efforts of the Frasers of Philorth. However, according to Cranna, the earliest settlement was probably at Kirkton (Kirktown) where the town's burial ground is now. The extension of the graveyard in 1866 unearthed the remains of shell middens which are indicative of a settlement site dating from any time between the Mesolithic period (c10,000 – 4,500 BC) and 19th century AD. In 1910, the probable footings of the pre-reformation parish church of Philorth were discovered just inside the inner gate of the cemetery. This church is known to have been in existence before 1274 and may have been built on the site of the chapel of St Modan, the patron saint of Fraserburgh, who probably chose this site because of its proximity to a settlement. The church remained in use until 1572 when it was replaced by a church in the new burgh closer to the Castle of Kinnaird, seat of Fraser of Philorth.

    The faintly Egyptian looking stone building with a stepped pyramidal roof topped by an obelisk, protruding above the cemetery dyke, is a 1933 reproduction of the original Saltoun Mausoleum in Saltoun Square.

A snowy day at Philorth Halt looking towards Rose Hill on the left and Corbie Hill on the right. The remains of the pedestrian gate of the level crossing can be seen on the lower left of the picture. This is the road which Lord Saltoun would have used between the halt and his house.

*Philorth Woods
seen from the
Halt*

Fraserburgh Golf Club (NK 003 653): Fraserburgh Golf Club claims to be the oldest golf club in the world still existing under its original name. Founded on 14 April 1777 by *'nineteen of the most prominent landed gentry in the north east of Scotland'*, the club is also the seventh oldest golf club in the world, the fifth oldest in Scotland and the oldest club north of St Andrews. The Parish Kirk Session is recorded as having disciplined a boy, John Burnett, for playing golf on the Sabbath in Fraserburgh in 1613.

Originally the course consisted of only nine holes and was situated on Fraserburgh Links. This course became overcrowded and play was frequently interrupted so, thanks to a gift of land from Lord Salton, the course moved to its present location in 1891. The present club house was opened in 2006, fire having destroyed its predecessor in 2004.

Rose Hill (NK 007 650) and Corbie Hill (NK 007 651): Writing in 1914 Cranna reports that *'old men living in Fraserburgh a generation or two ago, remembered that a brick and tile work was carried on at the Rosehill, the little hill which lies almost opposite the Corbiehill, on the Cairnbulg turnpike.'* The works would have used the clay which underlies the nearby bents. A house was built here in 1787 for the Philorth Estate pundlar who also seems to have operated a ferry boat on the Water of Philorth. The pundlar was employed to round up and impound straying cattle on the estate. Corbie Hill, directly beyond Rosehill, is named for the ravens which once flocked there.

Philorth Halt (NK 007 646): Philorth Halt was built and maintained by the railway company as a private station for Lord Saltoun as a condition of the line being able to pass through the Philorth Estate. Although Philorth opened in April 1865, it did not appear in public timetables until 1923 and was reserved for the exclusive use of Lord Saltoun, his family, mailbag and factor until 1926.

Latterly children of the estate workers travelled to school in Fraserburgh by train during the winter and on 'coorse' days in summer. Catching a train involved stepping out on to the platform and signalling by putting your arm out, like catching a bus today.

Close to the south end of the platform the railway line cut across the lane giving access to the Philorth Estate from the Fraserburgh – Cairnbulg Road. The honeysuckle clad remains of the level crossing gates and wooden pedestrians' gate have survived.

Philorth House and Estate (NK 002 641): The original Philorth House stands in extensive wooded policies and was built in 1666 by Sir Alexander Fraser, 10th Lord Saltoun, close to the former Saltoun seat of Cairnbulg Castle. He built the mansion, which became the seat of the Frasers of Philorth, on land which was part of his home farm, then known as Bungyietoun. Shortly afterwards the name was changed to Philorth. (Bungyietoun seems to be derived from the Gaelic *'buidhe'* meaning yellow, possibly from the gorse and lesser celandines which abound there, and *'toun'* Scots for farm.) Philorth House underwent several renovations and alterations and by 1876 had become an impressive L-plan house. Sadly it was almost completely destroyed by fire on the night of 25 March 1915. Although speculative gossip blamed the German butler, the fire was probably caused by a beam catching fire. The blaze, fanned by the strong north east winds spread rapidly, engulfing the newer part of the building and destroying it in about two hours. Servants from the Home Farm fought to quench the fire using buckets of water from a pond about 500 metres away. They were soon joined by people from Fraserburgh but it became apparent that all that could usefully be done was to prevent the fire reaching the private gas supply and to rescue furniture, family portraits and other valuables from the house. Lady Saltoun, the only member of the family present at the time, directed this operation. The Fire Brigade arrived from Fraserburgh but was unable to use its fire engine because of the impossibility of getting sufficient water. The fire did an estimated £25,000 of damage before burning itself out at about 2.30 a.m. A smaller, replacement house was subsequently built close to the ruined shell.

Cairnbulg Castle (NK 016 639): What is now Cairnbulg Castle was originally known as the Manor Place of Philorth, later becoming Philorth Castle, from its position close to the Water of Philorth. The castle was probably built in the 13th century by the Comyns, Earls of Buchan, as a defence against Norse invaders. When the castle was built it was close to the shore. However, over the centuries the sea has receded and the dune system between Fraserburgh and Cairnbulg Point has grown leaving the castle stranded inland. An old print shows boats beached on the shore very close to the castle mound. The original castle was destroyed by Robert the Bruce during the 'Harrying of Buchan' before being granted to the Earls of Ross. It passed into Fraser hands as part of a dowry when Joanna, daughter of the 5th Earl of Ross, married Sir Alexander Fraser of Cowie in 1375. Sir Alexander became the first Fraser Laird of Philorth and restored the castle as his family seat. The huge square tower which still dominates the castle was built at this time. Enlarged and altered many times over the centuries, by the mid-sixteenth century the building had become a Z-plan castle with two towers, one rectangular and one circular, at diagonally opposite corners of a central block. By 1613 Sir Alexander Fraser, 8th Laird of Philorth, who had spent vast amounts of money developing the town of Fraserburgh was bankrupt and was forced to sell the castle to a kinsman, Fraser of Durris. It was a condition of the original sale that Sir Alexander Fraser, or his descendants, would have the right to buy back the castle should it ever come on the market. Despite this agreement and a lawsuit, the attempts by his descendant the 10th Lord Saltoun to repurchase the castle in 1663 failed. In

The fourteenth century main tower of Cairnbulg Castle. This is one of the oldest buildings in Aberdeenshire still lived in by the family who built it.

1666 Lord Saltoun built Philorth House nearby at Bungyietoun which for centuries became the seat of the Frasers of Philorth.

Cairnbulg Castle, as it was known from the mid-17th century, changed hands several times. Between 1775 and 1801 it was owned by the Earl of Aberdeen who used stone from the castle for other building projects. In 1863 the remains of the castle were bought by Mr Duthie, an Aberdeen shipbuilder and tea clipper owner. In 1896 major restoration and rebuilding was carried out by his nephew, Sir John Duthie, largely using his wife's tocher (dowry) which he usefully received from her stone merchant father in the form of granite. However, in 1934 Alexander Fraser, 19th Lord Saltoun, purchased Cairnbulg Castle and it once again became the Fraser of Philorth family seat. Since then the castle has been extensively modernised and is now the home of The Hon. Mrs Kate Nicolson, eldest daughter of the 20th Lady Saltoun. It is not open to the public except by written appointment.

Milltown of Cairnbulg (NK 013 633): The Line crosses a small farm road and what was once a mill lade at Milltown of Cairnbulg. When the lease of Milltown of Cairnbulg, then part of the Philorth Estate, was due to expire the farm was described in the *Aberdeen Journal* for Wednesday 8 July 1812, as *'lying in a centrical situation, and in a fertile district of the country; within a few miles of the town and Harbour of Fraserburgh, and about thirteen from Peterhead, to both which towns, as well as to Aberdeen, there are good turnpike roads going through the Estate. The Lands are entitled to take Sea Ware and Shell Sand from the shore of Cairnbulg, where there is abundance of these manures, as well as an easy access of procuring dung from the fishing village, and the towns above-mentioned.'*

Gash of Philorth Doocot (NK 001 627): The tall stone tower visible just beyond Mains of Philorth Farm and the trees of the Philorth Estate is Gash of Philorth Doocot which was built around 1800. This octagonal dovecot is built of rough stone and dressed granite; there is a plain rectangular doorway with an oval panel above it and oval pigeon ports to give the birds access. Protruding 'rat courses' between the stages of the tower form landing ledges for the pigeons and prevent rats climbing in. The inside walls are lined with brick nesting boxes; a revolving ladder or potence in the centre of the doocot enabled eggs and young birds to be collected from the boxes. Only landowners with extensive estates were allowed to build doocots and harsh penalties existed for anyone stealing pigeons or their eggs. Before the introduction of agricultural improvements such as turnip growing, which allowed cattle to be over wintered in Buchan, pigeons provided an important source of food, particularly during winter months when meat was scarce. However, once livestock could be fed over the winter, the popularity of pigeon meat fell and there was an increasing resentment of the damage that pigeons did to neighbouring farmers' crops so doocots began to fall out of use.

Rathen Station (NK 016 624): Isolated Rathen Station, 1¼ miles beyond Philorth Halt, is now a house. It is over a mile from the rural hamlet of Rathen and nearly 3 miles from the fishing communities of Cairnbulg, Inverallochy and St Combs, all of which it served.

Prior to the opening of the St Combs Light Railway in 1903 it was not unusual for between 60 and 70 creel carrying fishwives to walk from Inverallochy, Cairnbulg and St Combs to Rathen Station. They travelled inland on the first southbound train of the day to country districts where they bartered their fish for farm produce such as eggs, butter and cheese. A Rathen guard described them as being *'Fully loaded baith wyes'*.

Rathen village is reached from the station by a sandy track which ascends Gallows Hill before dropping down to the ancient ruins of St Ethernan's Church (NK 001 609). The name Rathen may be a corruption of the saint's name or may be from the Gaelic for a round fort on a stream.

St Ethernan (or Eddran) is thought to have been a Pict of noble birth who studied religion in Ireland during the sixth century. Returning to Scotland he established several religious settlements before eventually reaching the Rathen area. Here he lived as a hermit in a cave, at St Eddran's Slack, on the East side of Mormond Hill and was befriended by a deer which remained close to his cell until his death on 2 December 669 AD. The corpse road from Strichen, over which bodies were carried for burial at Rathen, descends to St Eddran's Churchyard through the slack. The old kirkyard contains an attractive church ruin with the date 1646 on the south

Rathen Kirkyard, with the ruins of St Ethernan's Church.

aisle and an elegantly carved sandstone panel recording the patronage of Alexander Fraser of Philorth. There are two curious sandstone gargoyles and an unusual diamond shaped wall sundial dated 1625, alas lacking a gnomon. The great-great-grandparents of the Norwegian composer Edvard Grieg, who farmed in Rathen, are buried in the graveyard. Edvard Grieg's ancestor, Alexander Greig, emigrated from Scotland to Bergen where he worked in the British Consul's Office. It is said that he continued to cross the North Sea in a fishing boat twice yearly to attend communion in Rathen. The new church adjacent to the ruin was built in 1868.

Knockmonean Cairn (NK 017 622): Knockmonean Cairn, a large elongated pile of boulders and earth overgrown with gorse, dominates the hilltop to the east of the Line immediately after the junction with the unclassified Rathen to Gowanhill road. The cairn dates from the Neolithic period and is likely to have been built as a tomb by the first farmers in the area. Despite having been badly plundered, the cairn is about 50 metres long, 10 metres wide and 11 metres high and is now home to a multitude of rabbits.

Craigellie (NK 024 602): The estate consists of wooded policies and farmland. At its heart is the two storey mansion house, Craigellie House, designed by John Smith around 1840 and built in an elegant Italianate style. There is an extensive walled garden, the walls of which are visible from the Line when the surrounding trees are leafless.

HMS Merganser (NK 065 585): The 300 metre high antennae masts of the former Crimond naval air base station, officially HMS *Merganser*, are seen from several points along this section of the Line. The masts remain functional and are situated on Ministry of Defence property close to the Loch of Strathbeg.

HMS *Merganser* (also known as Rattray) was built in 1944 as a base for the Fleet Air Arm. It had four runways and was capable of housing around 3,000 personnel. *Merganser* was used at different periods during the Second World War as a base for Torpedo bombers, reconnaissance, observer, telegraphist and air gunner training. Fairey Barracuda aircraft, which were notoriously difficult to handle, were extensively used on the base resulting in several accidents. According to local tradition at least one ill-fated Barracuda is submerged in Strathbeg. The base was operational until 1946 and by 1976 was being used as a Royal Naval Radio Station.

Spillarsford Mill (NK 016 592): Close to the Line a little to the north of the A90 crossing, a group of ruins, inhabited until the 1970s, was a mill, reached by a track running across the fields from Spillarsford.

The beautifully detailed 1870 1st Edition 25 inch to the mile OS map shows the mill wheel in position on the gable end of the lower building. A small body of water close to the buildings, probably the mill dam and the mill lade, running under the bridge over the Line are also shown. The mill is not thought to have operated on a commercial scale, more probably grinding grain from the now demolished neighbouring farm.

Cortes Village or Spillarsford Cottages (NK 014 591): Clustered by the bridge over the Ellie burn on the Peterhead to Fraserburgh turnpike this small settlement was previously known as Spillarsford Cottages from a nearby farm but is now also known as Cortes Village. Cortes House is about half a mile to the west of the village.

The 1870 OS map shows a small cluster of cottages at Spillarsford including a poorhouse and Station Cottage, the home of the Lonmay Station agent. The poor house (now Bridge View and named for the long gone bridge carrying the railway line over the A90) served Rathen parish, being on the Rathen side of the Ellie Burn, the boundary between Rathen and Lonmay. This locally administered poorhouse was established by 1860 but became defunct by around 1900, by which time the Buchan Combination Poorhouse had been built at Maud.

Crimonmogate (NK 038 587): Crimonmogate takes its name from a combination of Gaelic and Old Norse words which mean 'road through the pasture by the peat moss' – said to refer to an ancient track across the estate which originally formed part of the vast lands owned by the Earl of Erroll. The Greek revival mansion house, designed by Archibald Simpson, was commissioned in 1820 by Patrick Milne, a highly successful businessman, whose enormous wealth was the result of enterprises in the West Indies, India and China. Milne died before the completion of the house in 1825 and it passed firstly to his relation Sir Charles Bannerman. His son Sir Alexander Bannerman planted extensive woodlands and trees throughout the policies which now make Crimonmogate a foremost sporting estate. Crimonmogate eventually became Erroll property again when it was inherited by Major Raymond Alexander Carnegie and his wife, the Countess of Erroll. Sasha Carnegie's book *Pigs I Have Known*, describes a post war pig keeping venture at Crimonmogate.

During World War 2 members of the Consolidated Pneumatic Tool Company head office staff were evacuated from London to Fraserburgh and were billeted at Crimonmogate and nearby Cairness.

Crimonmogate, the Greek revival mansion house, designed by Archibald Simpson, dates from the early nineteenth century.

Christopher Monckton, an adviser to Margaret Thatcher and inventor of the board game 'Eternity', lived here from 1996 to 2000. Monckton offered a prize of £1, 000,000 for what he thought was his virtually insoluble board game. Alas, the game was solved within a period of months by students using a computer and the house had to be sold.

In 2001 Crimonmogate was purchased by Lord and Lady Petersham, who carried out extensive restoration and now run a successful wedding and corporate events business from the property. The house may be visited by appointment only.

Lonmay Station (NK 014 586): Lonmay Station served a district of scattered farms and houses and was convenient for the estates of Crimonmogate and Cortes. In the season shooting parties bound for Crimonmogate alighted at Lonmay where there was a large turning area outside the station to accommodate their coaches and carriages. Monthly fairs were held near the station; the large imposing building on the road by the station was the local bank. Lonmay Post Office, which had been established at Cortes close to the junction of the turnpikes from Mintlaw and Peterhead to Fraserburgh in 1858, was relocated when the station opened.

The Statistical Accounts indicate that the district contained extensive bog which was laboriously reclaimed to produce agricultural land. During the 19th century seaweed, carted from the shores at Cairnbulg and St Combs, was used as an effective fertiliser producing good quality land particularly suited for growing the early potatoes for which the area is still noted. The 3rd Statistical Account (1960) records the production of seed potatoes in the area for export to England and South Africa.

The ancestors of Elvis Presley came from the Lonmay area. The first Presley recorded in America was Andrew Presley, a blacksmith and exiled Jacobite supporter, who arrived in North Carolina in 1745. His father, also Andrew, had married Elspeth Leg in Lonmay in 1713. A new tartan, Presley of Lonmay, was designed to celebrate the connection between 'The King' and Lonmay. The tartan is woven in four colours, blue for Peterhead (the Blue Toon), grey for the Buchan skies, green for grass and yellow for the cornfields of the area. Occasionally an Elvis look-alike may be seen incongruously wandering the area.

Cairness House (NK 038 609): The imposing classical granite facade of Cairness House can best be seen when walking towards Fraserburgh from Lonmay Station. According to *The Howes o' Buchan*, '*The building which has some pretentions both to age and beauty was built from the designs of (James) Playfair and finished in 1799. The architecture is Grecian and it is said that above £25,000*

The imposing mansion of Cairness House is conspicuous on the skyline from the vicinity of Lonmay Station.

was expended in its erection. The main structure is of greenstone, quarried in Rora; but the porch is of Cairngall granite. The building was erected by Charles Gordon, Esq of Buthlaw....The interior of the house is a perfect specimen of art.' The building of the 42 roomed mansion house was largely financed by the income from the Gordon's plantations in Jamaica.

The front of the house, visible from several points on the Line, is quite austere; a central block with pedimented porch and imposing steps is flanked by taller pavilions. Behind this neoclassical frontage is a semi-circular courtyard of offices so that the ground plan forms CH representing Cairness House. The courtyard contains a circular ice house. Extraordinary architectural features of the house include the cast iron chimney pots in the shape of fluted Doric columns and the Masonic arches on the pavilions.

Internally the house, which has recently been restored, contains many Grecian influenced designs and Masonic symbols: it is thought that the Egyptian Room was used for Masonic meetings. This room, the most astonishing feature of the house, is decorated with pseudo hieroglyphs and Masonic symbolism. It has been suggested that Playfair, who died whilst working on the house, is buried beneath the floor of this extraordinary room.

The distinguished Greek historian, Major General Thomas Gordon of Cairness and Buthlaw, was born at Cairness in 1788, inheriting the estate when he was 8 years old. Following a brief career in the Scots Greys he left the British Army and travelled extensively in Eastern Europe, including Greece, before serving in the Russian and Hanoverian Armies. Gordon was an outstanding Greek scholar and historian, carrying out meticulous archaeological excavations and publishing his respected two volume *History of the Greek Revolution* in 1832. When he retired to Cairness, Thomas Gordon developed the gardens, planting hundreds of ornamental trees; his original tree planting was re-created in 2002 to commemorate the Queen's Golden Jubilee.

Mormond Hill (NJ 970 570): Mormond Hill, was formed when great pressure and heat within the earth's crust metamorphosed soft sandstone into hard quartz which had a greater resistance to erosion than the surrounding rocks. Now much embellished, Mormond Hill is visible from almost all of the Line between Fraserburgh and Strichen, its two linked summits, Mormond and Waughton, rise above the Buchan plain to a height of about 230 metres. The collective name for both summits, Mormond, comes from the Gaelic, *'Mor'* big and *'monadh'* hill but may also be interpreted as meaning the sea hill.

Cortes Stag (NJ 986 569): Mormond Hill is thought to be the only Scottish hill decorated with hill carvings; two large figures, a horse and stag, both visible from the Line, are cut into the turf exposing the quartz below. The most recent of these carvings is the Cortes Stag which was cut into the hillside in November 1870 to commemorate the wedding of the Laird, Mr F.W. Cordiner. The stag is an emblem of Clan Fraser but it may also reflect the legend St Eddran's deer. (See Rathen above.) The 80 metre long stag, covering about an acre, consists of an outline filled with quartz stones. During the Second World War the stag was camouflaged by having brushwood and heather laid over it but this was burned during a moorland fire in 1944. The stag was restored to its pre-war glory in the summer of 1946 by a group of internees from Stuartfield POW camp.

North Atlantic Radar System (NJ 984 560): The masts and dishes on the summit of Mormond are the relics of Station 44, part of the North Atlantic Radar System. This early warning system developed by NATO during the Cold War, comprised a chain of detection points stretching from Fylingdales in Yorkshire to Iceland and was designed to give early warning of enemy missile launches. Station 44 was functional from 1961 until 1992 when the site was taken over by the Ministry of Defence. The earlier huge 'saucers' (radio dishes) have been removed but masts and underground structures remain and are now, reputedly, used by British Telecom and commercial radio stations and provide links to North Sea Oil platforms.

New Leeds (NJ 996 546): The hamlet of New Leeds came about as an ambitious but ill-conceived attempt, by Captain Alexander Fraser of the King's Dragoon Guards, to transform the district known as Whig-About, then regarded as the haunt of thieves and smugglers, into a woollen producing town to rival its Yorkshire namesake. However, the proposed settlement never prospered. Unlike at Strichen, founded by Captain Fraser's father, no housing was

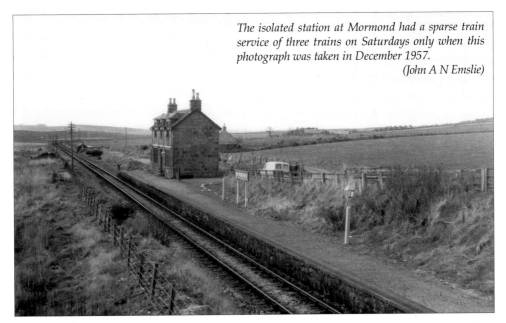

The isolated station at Mormond had a sparse train service of three trains on Saturdays only when this photograph was taken in December 1957.

(John A N Emslie)

offered to prospective settlers and the first inhabitants were reduced to living in wooden shacks. Eventually stone cottages were built for the weavers; a market and occasional fairs were established by 1799 when the laird offered a prize for the drunkest man at the market. This rather set the tone for the community although a church, hall and shops were gradually set up and respectability was achieved.

The original name of the settlement Whig-About, is derived from the Old Scots word '*whig*' meaning to jog on a horse, incidentally the same derivation as the political party which became the core of the Liberal Party.

A notable native of New Leeds was James Rollo Duncan, born in 1859, the son of a farm worker and unknown father. Raised by his aunt, James Rollo Duncan emigrated to Bolivia and amassed great wealth as a tin magnate. On his return to Scotland he was able to build Tillycorthie mansion and much of the village of Udny Station.

Mormond Station (NJ 985 559): Under the shadow of Mormond Hill, 2½ miles from Strichen station, Mormond boasts a two storey station house, built after the owner of the original station house failed to renew the lease. The station chiefly served New Leeds and the estate of Park but attracted so little use that, as early as 1890, when the lease on the first station house expired, closure was contemplated. However a new station house, similar to the one at Newseat, was built and the reprieved station retained its goods service until June 1940 when it became solely a passenger station. In the 1820s the Park district was the base of Messrs Willox, carriers who dominated the carrying trade in Buchan and were reputedly the only Buchan company to have regular trade with London. The company, like many others, declined as a result of the efficiency, economy and speed of the railway freight service.

The White Horse (NJ 962 566): The most credible of the many theories about the origin of the white horse which is such a distinctive landmark on Mormond Hill is that it was created at the behest of Captain Fraser, son of Lord Strichen, on his return from serving in the King's Dragoon Guards during the French Revolutionary Wars. On 26 August 1794, during a battle against the French at Glize in Holland, Captain Fraser's horse was shot from beneath him. Sergeant James Hutcheon, a crofter's son from New Pitsligo, gave his horse to Captain Fraser saying that he could easily find a mount for himself from amongst the rider-less horses. Unfortunately, the sergeant was killed before he could find a new horse. It is thought that Captain Fraser had seen the Uffington white horse and was inspired by this to have the Mormond Horse cut as a memorial to Hutcheon. A brass plaque removed from Mormond Church, now in Strichen Library, commemorates Sergeant Hutcheon. Alternative theories are that the horse was a war

The white horse on Mormond Hill. The hill has what are thought to be the only two hill carvings in Scotland, the white horse and the Cortes stag, both of which can be seen from the Formartine and Buchan Way as it passes round the lower slopes of Mormond.

memorial cut by the Strichen estate tenants around 1820, that it commemorates the visit of Dr Johnson to Strichen House in 1770 or, less feasibly, that it commemorates Lord Strichen driving a carriage and pair over the hill. The horse was covered in turf during World War 2 to prevent it being used as a landmark by enemy aircraft but is now regularly cleaned and maintained by volunteers from Strichen.

Mormond Hill Hunters' Lodge (NJ 965 567): The ruined two storey hunting lodge built around 1779 by Captain Fraser, stands on the skyline of Mormond Hill above the white horse. An inscription above the lintel reads: '*In this Hunter's Lodge Rob Gibb commands, MDCCLXXIX.*' According to a slightly confused local tradition Rob Gibb was a locally born court jester to either King James V (1513 - 1542), James VI or Charles II who reputedly said "*I serve your Majesty for stark love and kindness*". However, the name 'Robb Gibb 'was used as a covert Jacobite toast, so it is probable that the inscription was a political statement in support of Charles Edward Stewart within whose lifetime the lodge was built.

The ground floor of the Lodge consisted of a single room, used by the laird and his guests after a day's hunting on the hill. The fireplace was said to be large enough to roast a deer. The upstairs provided accommodation for the estate gamekeeper and his family. The lodge, claimed one keeper, was haunted and the keeper's salary was regularly increased in line with the severity of the hauntings. The lodge was inhabited until the early 19th century.

Mormond Hill and the Hunting Lodge served as a landmark for sailors and is commemorated in the mariners' rhyme, '*Keep Mormond Hill a handspike high and Rattray Briggs ye'll not come nigh*'. Rattray Briggs is a particularly treacherous sea area of rocks and reefs between Fraserburgh and St Combs, to be avoided at all costs.

Dencallie Farm (NJ 967 558): Before the parish of Strichen was created, coffins were carried along the corpse road over Mormond Hill for burial at Rathen about 9 miles away. Mourners used the route over the hill in order to avoid the marshy lower ground. Part of this track is still marked by stones, known as lych or resting stones, thought to mark places where the coffin was laid down so that teams of bearers could change over. Not all corpses appear to have completed the journey to Rathen; a Strichen estate map dated 1760 marks the '*Place where three men has been buried*' in a marshy area close to the corpse road. The 'Font Stone' situated at the half way point is where the Rathen minister would meet parents from Strichen who brought children for baptism.

A large cairn, probably dating from the Bronze Age, known as the Resting Cairn, suggesting an association with the corpse road, is above Dencallie which derives its name from the Gaelic for the Den of Rest.

Thomas the Rhymer, a 13th century prophet from the Scottish Borders, made two predictions about Mormond, both of them involving Dencallie. The first that, '*Mormond Hill should be carried to the sea*' is said to have been fulfilled when in July 1789 a huge waterspout carried great quantities of turf and heather from the den above Dencallie to the Ugie and eventually into the sea at Peterhead. The second prophecy stated that '*Dencaldie's Den (sic) should run in bluid*'. This had a clause which said that '*should the price of salt rise above the price of oatmeal this prediction would fall to the ground*'. Fortunately disaster was indeed averted by a steep rise in the price of oatmeal.

Howford (NJ 953 548): Howford, locally known as 'Howie's' or 'The French House', is to the south of the Line close to the intersection with the B9093. The rather imposing new house replaced the early 19th century farmhouse, built for Louis Servan, a French émigré. This building is currently a much decayed ruin, used as a store, but still showing its former elegance. Built in a French style, its rounded corners, arched windows, tiny pavilions and back courtyard are in complete contrast to the traditional foursquare granite farmhouses of Buchan.

Quite how Louis Servan arrived in Strichen remains enigmatic. Little definite is known of him, beyond that he is buried in Strichen kirkyard and, as his gravestone records, died aged 80 on 8 December 1834. His first wife, Mary Black died on 8 March 1814. Servan was survived by his second wife, Mary Keith. Mrs C.J. Thomson suggests in *Around the White Horse* that Servan may have fled France during the Revolution (1789-1799). One theory is that Howford was built for Servan by Lord Strichen as reward for an act of valour on the battlefield.

Locally known as the 'French Farm' the old farmhouse at Howford was built in the early nineteenth century for Louis Servan, a French émigré and is very different in style from the more usual foursquare Buchan farmhouses of the period.

Since 1994 Howford has been home to a highly successful training centre for adults with special needs. The centre supplies kindling and wood for wood burning stoves and in the spring and summer the horticultural area sells a wide range of plants, raised on site so fully acclimatised to conditions in Buchan.

The humpbacked Howford Bridge, adjacent to the farm, was built in 1777 to carry the Peterhead to Banff coach road over the Ugie, replacing an earlier footbridge and ford. Prior to the construction of the Turnpike the coach from Peterhead to Banff took 13 hours, including a 3 hour rest, to complete the return journey.

Strichen Toll House (NJ 949 550): Following the Turnpike Act of 1795, local Turnpike Trusts consisting of landowners and burghers whose estates exceeded £400 Scots, were able to apply for an Act of Parliament empowering them to build roads, in some cases by raising statute labour, and to levy tolls to pay for their construction and maintenance. The Act stipulated that the roads had to be built and maintained to a high standard; the Trustees, usually the landowners through whose estates the road was to pass, recovered their costs by renting out the right to collect tolls from travellers.

The right to collect tolls was usually let annually by auction to prospective Toll Keepers who balanced the likely income from tolls against the price paid for the right to collect them. Toll houses, usually two roomed cottages, often with a rounded or angled gable end allowing the toll keeper to see travellers approaching from both directions, were built every six miles. Outside the toll house a barrier with a counter balanced bar (the 'turnpike') blocked the road until the toll had been paid.

Charges varied from locality to locality and for different types of wheeled transport or animal traffic. Herds of beasts were charged by the score but carts which had passed through the toll point when loaded were usually exempt when they returned empty. Only trips of less than 200 yards, and by the 1850s funeral processions and pedestrian mourners, were exempt from tolls. Mail coaches were exempt from paying at individual toll houses but paid an annual fee. When a mail coach approached a toll house the guard would sound his trumpet to warn the toll keeper to allow the mail coach through unhindered. Turnpike Trusts were seldom profitable. Their death knell was the completion of the railway which drastically reduced the amount of road traffic and resulted in the removal of all Aberdeenshire toll bars in 1866.

Shunting in progress at Strichen in May 1949 when the goods train for Fraserburgh called there. Wagons could run by gravity into the sidings but it was more of a struggle to bring them out again on a damp day. Strichen was one of the busier stations on the line.   *(G H Robin)*

Strichen Station (NJ 949 549): Strichen Station was the only intermediate station on this branch of the Formartine & Buchan Railway to serve a town. Work on the Strichen section of the line began in August 1863. Immediately after the ceremonial cutting of the first sod and a celebratory beer *'over 200 sturdy looking fellows manned with vigour the planks, shovels and barrows,'* and began construction. An interesting first-hand account of the changes the railway brought to Strichen is given in *Around the White Horse*, the memoirs of Mrs C. J. Thomson, formerly Miss Charlotte Jane Gavin of Holmwood House, Strichen, written in 1888, just 23 years after the railway arrived in Strichen.

'This pleasant view (to the West of the town) down the valley of the Ugie is cut off now by the railway embankment, built in 1865, but in exchange for the amenity of a pleasant prospect, there are the practical advantages of easy ingress and egress to and from the village with facilities for traffic which largely promote the prosperity of the people.

'There are two banks in the village and a monthly market. The railway does good service on these occasions, bringing the country folk by noon and carrying them off again to their homes by four o'clock p.m. so that scenes of drunkenness are a thing of the past; all is quiet before evening as if no market had been.'

Born in 1811 Miss Gavin was the sixth daughter of Dr Alexander Gavin of Strichen, who is often credited with having written the popular bothy ballad, 'Mormond Braes'. This tells the story of a jilted Strichen lass's determination to make the best of her situation, and celebrates the Buchan virtues of stoic tenacity and upbeat optimism despite setbacks.

> *For I'll gang doon tae Strichen toon,*
> *Where I wis bred and born,*
> *An there I'll get another sweethert,*
> *That'll marry me the morn.*
>
> *So fare ye weel ye Mormond Braes,*
> *Where oft times I've been cheery,*
> *Mormond Braes where heather grows,*
> *For it's there I lost my dearie.*

Rev J R Calder, recorded in the *Third Statistical Account* for Strichen that the words of 'Mormond Braes' used to be printed in full on the paper bags used in at least one grocer's shop in Strichen.

Mormond Parish Church (NJ 947 547): Prior to the improvement and renaming of the village by Lord Strichen, the settlement was known as Mormond Village and was probably clustered round the original Mormond Parish Church. All that now remains of this church, built around 1620 at the expense of the laird, Thomas Fraser, on high ground above the Ugie, is the laird's burial aisle. As a result of the efforts of Lord Strichen, Thomas Fraser's great grandson, to develop the town, the church became too small for the expanding community. Around 1799 a new, larger parish church, dedicated to St Andrew, was built in the graveyard to the south of the first church. The original church is reputed to have then been used to lock up criminals. St Andrews Church was in turn abandoned in 1961.

Strichen Market Stance (NJ 947 549): William Anderson in *The Howes o' Buchan* eulogised the town: *'Strichen which is without exception, the most attractive and picturesque spot on the whole line. Lying in a snug little valley, with the towering crest of Mormond on the one side, the limpid waters of the Ugie on the other, and embowered among trees - Strichen is, without doubt, one of the prettiest little villages in Buchan.'*

Strichen, one of the best examples in Aberdeenshire of a planned village, was founded in 1764 by the Honourable Alexander Fraser, 7th Lord Strichen. Like other improving Lairds of the time, he was anxious to develop a centre of manufacturing and industry on his estate so made feus available on the lower slopes of Mormond Hill. An advertisement in the *Aberdeen Journal* for 21 November 1763 claimed, *'plenty of stone, lime and inexhaustible moss, a weekly market and four great fairs annually; the situation is within 6 miles of 9 fishtowns and would be a most convenient receptacle for all persons concerned in the linen manufactureys, as there is plenty of yarn already spun in the country.'* The settlement rapidly flourished owing to the generous 'start up terms' offered to new settlers. According to Rev William Anderson, writing in the *Statistical Account of Scotland*, incentives included *'giving a premium for erecting a lint mill and distributing lint seed gratis; but most effectively by the establishment of a yarn market which holds at the beginning of March and middle of May, at which the capital manufacturers and dealers attend; and the country people are not only sure of a sale, and ready money, but of the highest price their yarn is worth. The Trustees gave a premium of £5 per annum for five years to the person who purchased the greatest quantity of yarn made from flax of the growth of the country. This occasioned a competition among the buyers in which the sellers found their advantage, so that these markets, where there used not to be a single spindle disposed of, upwards of 4,000 spindles have been sold for some years past by the country people.'*

To ensure that there was no delay in establishing the town Lord Strichen offered a prize for the first settlers to have built a house with *'a reeking lum'*. By 1797 Mormond was a post town receiving mail three times each week, the textile industry was prospering with watermills powered by the Ugie processing locally grown flax, meal and wool. There were five fairs for the sale of horses and cattle each year. An annual market for the sale of locally produced linen yarn was held every February until the linen trade declined in the 1800s. The town was renamed Strichen around 1850, a recumbent grave slab dated 1842 in the kirkyard has the original name 'Mormond.'

The markets held on the market stance, now the empty green area east of the viaduct, continued to be of great importance to the village economy. Pedlars and fishwives, whose range was extended by the arrival of the railway, would visit bringing a wider range of goods to Strichen. Twice yearly 'feein' markets were traditionally held on the first Wednesdays after 19 May and 12 November and by the 19th century a cattle market was also held on the first Thursday of every month. The weekly Tuesday market survived until the 1950s.

In a paper entitled 'The History of Strichen', delivered to the Buchan Field Club in 1891 Robert Anderson records that two whale bones used to stand in the Market Stance close to the railway line. These bones were used as the town stocks and miscreants such as drunks were reputedly chained by the neck to the bones and subjected to public humiliation. Even more grisly was the nearby chair with a long pole attached to it – used to 'dook' those unfortunates

In early spring the damp ground on the banks of the Ugie, as it flows under Strichen viaduct, is thickly carpeted with wood anemones and celandines.

Situated on the corner of High Street and Bridge Street, Strichen's impressive Town House once housed a covered market on the ground floor. The steeple bell was rung at 6 a.m. each morning to wake the inhabitants of Strichen – and at 8 p.m. as a curfew.

accused of witchcraft in the Ugie.

Until recently the shell of the village's secondary school was close to the Line at the southern end of the stance. In the mid-1920s poetess Flora Garry, then Flora Campbell, taught English at the school and was considered by the pupils as being '*o'er bonny to be a teacher*'.

Strichen Viaduct (NJ 946 549): Strichen viaduct carries the Line high above the River Ugie close to the road bridge over the river on the southern edge of the town. The viaduct stands close to the site of a now forgotten mill, demolished prior to the construction of the railway. Building the viaduct was not without difficulty; in December 1864 when it was being built two of the supports of the bridge gave way. This caused a delay in the completion of the line and many navvies were laid off whilst it was rebuilt. The viaduct was reconstructed in 1922 when the main single span was replaced by three spans supported on high granite pillars. The town's gas works was situated on the north bank of the Ugie close to the viaduct.

Town House (NJ 947 552): The town hall building was gifted to the community by Mr Fraser of Strichen House in 1816. The spire and tower can be seen from the Line as it crosses the viaduct. McKean describes the tower and spire as being of 16th century Scots Tollbooth inspiration, whilst the adjoining hall block is classical. Originally the hall had an open arcade on the ground floor which was used as a covered market. The steeple contained a bell. Mrs Thomson recalls that before the steeple was built the inhabitants of Strichen were woken at 5 each morning by the Town Crier sounding a drum or, in foul weather, a horn. Curiously, once the Town Hall bell was operational the day began an hour later. The bell became the signal for the Town Crier, resplendent in his uniform, a red coat with blue piping, to begin his rounds announcing events of local importance. Until the late 1930s the bell was also rung at 8 p.m. as an evening curfew. For a time during the late 19th century a female school was held in the lower part of the building.

Strichen Parish Church (NJ 945 554): The spire of the present Parish Church, built in 1893, is at the end of High Street and can be seen from the viaduct. This church, originally a Free Church known as the North Church, became the parish church in 1932 when the parish minister died and the two congregations were united.

Strichen Community Park and Woodlands (NJ 944 550): Strichen Community Park is an attractive and well maintained amenity developed in the grounds of Strichen House as a result of the efforts of local people. The Lodge has been turned into an excellent cafe, opened in July 2011 by the then First Minister, Alex Salmond, himself a Strichen resident. There are several attractive walks in the woodlands and around the lake which originally powered a

Strichen Lodge, now a cafe in the Community Park.

nearby mill. Although this was demolished before the railway viaduct was built, the moss covered remains of the mill sluice can still be seen in the Community Park. The lake became an ornamental feature around 1820 when the grounds of Strichen House were landscaped.

The Lodge, it is claimed, was for a time the home of Strichen authoress, Lorna Moon. Born Helen (Nora) Low in 1886, she showed a literary and romantic bent from an early age, eloping from Strichen in 1907 with William Hebditch, a commercial traveller who visited the Temperance Hotel owned by her parents. The couple settled in Canada where Nora reinvented herself as Lorna and took up firstly with a journalist, Walter Moon, then after embarking on a Hollywood screenwriting career, with William de Mille, brother of Cecil. During the 1920s Lorna published a collection of short stories, *Doorways in Drumorty,* and a novel, *Dark Star,* which led to a career as a screen writer. The short stories reflected unfavourably on the concerns of a small Scottish town very like Strichen enabling some locals to recognise themselves in less than flattering pen portraits. Whilst working in Hollywood Lorna had a son, Richard, to William de Mille but abandoned the baby to the care of his father in order to follow

Close to the entrance to the Community Park the remains of the former railway bridge which carried the Line over the A981 were painted in 2014 with an attractive 'Welcome to Strichen' mural depicting the Mormond Hill white horse.

her glittering career. Lorna became the most successful and highly paid Hollywood screen writer of her generation. Following her death from tuberculosis in May 1930, her ashes were returned to Strichen and scattered on Mormond Hill by her father, Charles Lowe. Lorna's books caused outrage in Strichen and were banned for many years by Strichen Library. However her rehabilitation is now well under way with blue plaques on significant buildings and a Lorna Moon display in the library. A stage version of 'Doorways' is regularly performed throughout Scotland.

The Cloisters (NJ 941 550): According to Miss Gavin, The Cloisters on Brewery Road was built around 1851 by Captain Fraser of Strichen House. On his return from the travels of his youth he married a French lady, Miss Leslie of Bohine, a Roman Catholic for whom, although a Protestant himself, he built the Cloisters and attached Gothic chapel.

Strichen Stone Circle (NJ 936 544): At the west end of Newton Wood a bridge carries the Line over a burn and a signposted track leading to Strichen Stone Circle. The stone circle, situated on a hill top about ¼ mile from the Line has had a troubled history. The recumbent stone circle, dating from the 3rd to 2nd millennium BC, referred to by Dr Johnson in 1773 as a 'Druidical Temple', was cleared from its site by a zealous improving farmer around 1830 and at Lord Lovat's insistence reconstructed as 'a picturesque Druidical Grove' centred on an ancient horse chestnut tree. As recently as 1965 the circle was bulldozed during over enthusiastic tree felling. Between 1979 and 1983 the circle was excavated and reconstructed on the original site, as intended by its builders. A huge recumbent block of granite, characteristic of stone circles in the North East, is flanked by two uprights and would have been carefully manoeuvred into a horizontal position in line with the southern moonset. Shot holes, relics of the earlier attempts to use gunpowder to destroy it, scar the recumbent. The slight bank on which the stones sit contains a covering of quartzite flakes, flint arrow heads and remains of a cremation burial.

The round tower a short distance from the stone circle is a dovecot, reputedly also used as a prison.

Strichen Brewery (NJ 936 549): Little is known about the brewery. It appears in the Post Office Directory for 1847-8 when Donald Junor and Co were listed as farmers and brewers, by 1853 succeeded by Hugh Junor. In the Ordnance Survey Name Book 1865-1871 the brewery is described as being a small property adjoining the farm of Newmill belonging to George Baird, Esquire of Strichen House. When the railway line was being constructed a small quarry, now the site of a modern bungalow, was dug to the east of Newmill to provide stone for the construction of railway bridges etc. During quarrying several prehistoric urns, flint arrow heads and stone axes were discovered. After the closure of the brewery, by then merely a bottling plant, the stock of old bottles was dumped in the quarry.

Strichen stone circle – the recumbent stone flanked by two uprights is a characteristic of stone circles throughout the North East. The densest concentration of such circles in Britain occurs in the region.

Strichen House (NJ 936 542): The sadly despoiled ruins of Strichen House can be seen through the trees to the south of the Line about ½ mile west of the viaduct. Strichen House replaced an earlier mansion and was built in an elegant Grecian style in 1821 for Thomas Fraser, Lord Strichen, later Lord Lovat. The once elegant three storey building, constructed from granite quarried on the estate, had an imposing portico with fluted columns and was set in extensive landscaped grounds. In 1855 the estate was sold to the Bairds of Gartsherrie (of iron foundry fame), whose guests included actress Lillie Langtry, mistress of Edward VII. The house was subsequently used as a shooting lodge, rented at one point by Aberdonian opera singer Mary Garden. In 1925 the estate was sold off; a year later the house was bought by a group of English businessmen who converted it into an upmarket hotel locally known as 'The Hydro'. Despite

This overbridge south of Strichen is one of many on the Formartine and Buchan Way which have had to be repaired over the years. Here, great care was taken to retain the attractive Victorian ballustrade.
(Keith Fenwick)

boasting facilities including two tennis courts, a nine hole golf course and trout fishing in the lake the hotel functioned for only three years. During World War 2 the building was requisitioned for use as an army billet for troops from Poland, Norway and Britain. In 1947 it was de-requisitioned and by 1954 was unroofed and gutted so that all that now remains is a granite shell abutted by a clutter of corrugated iron agricultural buildings.

The estate was visited by Dr Johnson and Boswell during their tour of Scotland in 1773 when the visitors commented favourably on the mature trees in the grounds of Strichen House. Dr Johnson wrote that *'he had travelled 200 miles (in Scotland) and had only seen one tree not younger than himself, but at Strichen he saw trees of full growth, worthy of his notice.'*

Roman Catholic Chapel Ruin (NJ 931 545): The ecclesiastical ruin with empty window arches is the shell of a Roman Catholic Chapel which was only partially built then abandoned when Lord Strichen became the 14th Lord Lovat and with his Roman Catholic wife moved to Beauly. In the days of Strichen Hydro Hotel the area round the ruin was a golf course.

Brucklay Station (NJ 927 505): Brucklay derives from the word brock, a badger and arose because the hill on which Brucklay Castle, situated a little to the east of the station, stands was once known as Brocks Hillock; this became Brock's law and eventually Brucklay.

Brucklay Station, which housed a post office, served Brucklay Estate and New Pitsligo. The station was the scene of a fatal accident on 25 July 1889 when a passenger train heading to Aberdeen from Fraserburgh was running slightly late and was diverted to the middle goods siding by an inexperienced pointsman. Unfortunately the train crashed into a row of wagons in the siding instantly killing George Fowlie, an elderly crofter from the New Pitsligo district, as he unloaded wood. The engine of the train was damaged but the crew and most of the passengers were unhurt. A subsequent Board of Trade Accident enquiry found that the train driver had been on duty for 10 hours and the pointsman, who had only been employed for 23 days, had worked for 7 hours.

The modern bridge just to the west of the station carries the A950 over the Line and replaced an older road bridge demolished in January 2008. The section of walkway from the bridge to the outskirts of Maud was the last to be cleared and surfaced, opening as recently as autumn 2012.

Brucklay Castle (NJ 911 501): The ruinous shell of Brucklay Castle, also known as Brucklaw Castle, stands in around 60 acres of policies including mature woodlands, now a shooting estate.

The earliest buildings on the site belonged to the estate of Fedderate, Brucklay having been granted to the Laird of Fedderate's eldest son in the 15th century. The oldest part of the present building is the ruined tower house built by James Crawford, 1st Laird of Brucklay, around 1600 possibly on the site of earlier buildings. The original character of the building is hidden by the many alterations which took place before 1850 when the castle was transformed into a (reputedly) 100 roomed Victorian baronial mansion. The policies included a 5 acre garden containing formal terraces and a huge lake which took 12 years to dig using only buckets and spades. The castle was used as prisoner of war camp in World War 2; the prisoners lived in huts in grounds with officers billeted in the castle. The castle was unroofed around 1952.

The estate remained in Crawford hands for two centuries before passing briefly to the Irvines of Drum then, through a marriage in 1642, to Arthur Dingwall whose family eventually became Dingwall Fordyce. The Dingwall Fordyce family were well respected naval officers, politicians and lairds who did much to improve the conditions of their tenants.

In February 2004 a bizarre memorial pheasant shoot was held at Brucklay using cartridges which contained the ashes of the firearms expert whose life was being commemorated.

Culsh Monument (NJ 882 483): The conspicuous monument crowning the Hill of Culsh above New Deer is a well-known landmark built in 1876 to commemorate William Dingwall Fordyce of Brucklay Castle, the first MP for Aberdeenshire.

The 25 metre high ashlar monument overlooking Culsh Cemetery has an internal spiral staircase leading to the now inaccessible viewing platform directly below the spire. A Liberal MP, William Dingwall Fordyce was a benevolent laird who improved living conditions for his tenants, introduced insurance for their cottages and ran weekly carriages to Banff, Aberdeen and Peterhead. He was also influential in ensuring that the Buchan Railway was extended north beyond Ellon and that Brucklay Station was sited close to his seat, Brucklay Castle.

During the construction of the monument the remains of a prehistoric stone circle were removed and used in the foundations of the New Deer Manse.

Bertie Forbes, multimillionaire founder of the financial journal, *Forbes Magazine*, was born in 1880 at Whitehill close to New Deer, where his father was a tailor, and is now buried at

When the railway was in operation, huts were provided at intervals for the men who maintained the track. A ganger would regularly walk along the line to check that it was in good condition. These huts provided shelter and enabled materials to be stored ready for use. This example is at Atherb, near Brucklay.

Culsh Monument. Situated on the Hill of Culsh above New Deer the monument to William Dingwall Fordyce M.P. is conspicuous on the skyline when walking the Line between Brucklay and Maud.

Culsh. He died in 1954 and was buried in New York but 35 years later his body was reinterred here by his son. The grave of folksong collector Gavin Greig is also found here.

St Kane's New Deer (NJ 886 470): Looking west from the bridge over the South Ugie Water the majestic tower of New Deer Church can just be seen above the brow of the hill. The present church, built in 1839-1841, is dedicated to St Kane and is close to what is thought to be the site of a chapel established by the saint. The tower was added to the building in 1865.

Rev. Dr John B Pratt author of *Pratt's Buchan*, was born at Slacks of Cairnbanno near New Deer in 1796 and received his early education at the parish school there. *Buchan,* regarded as being one of the foremost Victorian examples of local history and topography guides, was first published in 1858 and in a facsimile edition in 1978.

Honeyneuk (NJ 920 486): The farm of Honeyneuk is set on a hillside overlooking Maud. The present farmhouse was built in 1910. The father of the author and journalist Jack Webster, who was for many years auctioneer at Maud mart, farmed the 200 acres of Honeyneuk from 1952 until his death in 1977.

In the mid-19th century a girls' school was set up at Honeyneuk by Miss Paterson, the farmer's daughter who firstly held classes in the front room of her house. However in 1838 James Mitchel, the Pitfour Estate factor, left money for the establishment and financing of schools for girls on the estate. Four schools including a new school at Honeyneuk, which opened in 1842, were built under the terms of the bequest. Eventually the girls' school was amalgamated with the boys' school at Bank and with Maud School when it opened on 29 April 1896.

Maud Church (NJ 927 478): The west gable of Maud Church and the bellcote which surmounts it can be seen from the Line on the approach to Maud. The church owes its existence to the growth of the community, then known as Bank, after the arrival of the railway. At first a mission station which used Bank school for services, was run by a missionary who was overseen by the Old Deer minister. As the population increased a church became necessary and it opened on 23 June 1876, partly funded by donations amounting to £1,100. In 1890 Maud became a separate parish and the missionary in charge since 1883, William Cowie, was ordained as the first minister – a position he held until 1918.

One of William Cowie's daughters, Mabel (1898 – 1975), became a well-known author writing 17 plays, 11 novels and 7 film scripts under the pen name of Lesley Storm. Most of her output dealt with marriage, family politics and the place of women in society, some being considered rather daring for a daughter of the manse. Her screenplays included Graham Greene's 'The Fallen Idol' (which starred Ralph Richardson and Jack Hawkins) and 'The Heart of the Matter'. 'Black Chiffon', her most famous stage play opened in London's West End in 1949, starring Flora Robson in the lead role; it ran to over 400 performances before moving to Broadway.

Maud (NJ 925 480): The growth of Maud was due to the eventual decision of the railway company to site the junction of the Peterhead and Fraserburgh sections of the railway there. This transformed the small hamlet of Bank of Behitch into a thriving, bustling community with the railway as its hub. According to local tradition Bank of Behitch was so called because it was where carters used to hitch up an extra horse to ease the load up the hill. The name is more likely to be derived from the Gaelic *cheithich* – a birch tree and is thought to predate even the use of carts.

With the establishment of the railway close to the hamlet a lively community rapidly began to develop as many of the new railway employees settled there. Monthly cattle fairs were already held in the area, but the presence of the railway enabled the mart to develop to become one of the largest in the country. This also increased openings for other workers, shopkeepers and craftsmen.

Easy access from across Buchan by train also led to the siting of the Buchan Combination Poorhouse in Maud which was central to the area served by the institution. This also further increased employment opportunities and contributed to the economic and population growth of the area.

Maud post office was established by 1895; prior to then the mail was delivered by an old lady who carried it from Old Deer, at the charge of a penny per item.

Maud Pill Box (NJ 926 479): A Second World War hexagonal granite pill box is situated close to the Line just outside Maud Station. It overlooks the road junction.

Maud Junction Station (NJ 926 479): At first the station was known as Brucklay but when the Fraserburgh line opened on 24 April 1865 that name was used for the next station down the line, closer to Brucklay Castle. The station was then rechristened New Maud after the nearby farms, Mill of Old Maud and Mains of Old Maud; however on 30 December 1867 the station

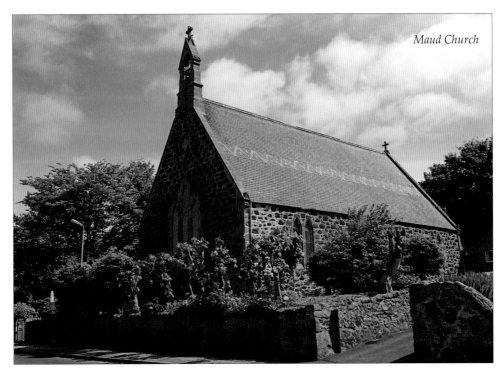

Maud Church

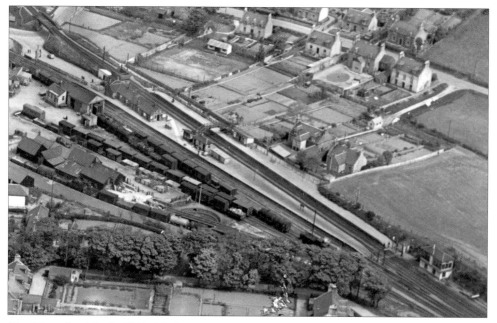

Maud from the air in the 1950s. The large number of wagons in the sidings reflect the heavy cattle traffic at that time, although it all transferred to road by the early 1960s. The line from Fraserburgh came in from the left, with the one from Peterhead just above it. The line south to Dyce and Aberdeen can be seen bottom right.
                                                                                          (Maud Museum)

was yet again renamed, this time as Maud Junction.

Maud Junction was an extremely busy station: it was here that trains from Aberdeen to Fraserburgh and Peterhead split into two sections. There was frenetic activity on mart days as cattle were loaded and unloaded in the sidings which were gradually enlarged to cope with the expanding mart traffic.

The status of the station as a junction and the need to split and merge trains was reflected in its layout. The branch lines to Peterhead and Fraserburgh converged south of the island platform and there were extensive goods yards and loading bays for cattle to the west of the lines. The wall of the engine turntable remains in the station yard. The station building on the island platform fronted the Peterhead side of the platform; the Fraserburgh side was unadorned. A footbridge was added to give access to the up Peterhead platform in 1882, where a small shelter was provided. A kitchen and refreshment rooms were added to the north end of the station building in 1869 to cater for the large numbers of people attending the mart. These were privately run, had an excellent reputation and did a roaring trade on mart days when the platform water tower was put to good use by the 'refresh' staff to cool bottles of beer. Sadly the water tower was also used by two suicides who drowned there in 1912 and 1913.

In January 1862 the *Peterhead Sentinel* reported that a special train had been run to Brucklay Station (Maud Junction) to convey dealers and animals to the mart. After the sale 146 cattle and 40 sheep, which amounted to about half the animals traded that day, were transported to Aberdeen by train. This marked the beginning of a huge growth in the volume of cattle passing through Maud as the railway permitted the fast, efficient movement of livestock thus widening the market available to north east farmers. By 1895 there were three Wednesday marts in Maud – at its peak the largest fatstock sale in Britain, dispatching beasts to destinations across Scotland and England, notably Glasgow, London and Liverpool. The number of fat cattle passing through the mart was seasonal, May and June being the peak period.

Hundreds of very young calves arrived each week. Individual calves tied up in sacks and travelling in the guard's van were the surplus of the Devon, Somerset and South Wales dairy industries. Larger quantities were transported in horse boxes or cattle wagons attached to trains travelling from Aberdeen to Fraserburgh and uncoupled at Maud. In 1985, even though

A recent aerial view of Maud. The station building in the centre now houses the Maud Railway Museum. The goods yard has been replaced by a car park, while the area to the south of the station is heavily wooded. The remains of the turntable can just be seen middle right.   *(Cabro Aviation Ltd)*

the number of animals passing through the mart was starting to decline as farms amalgamated and arable farming increased, the mart handled 21,136 store cattle; 6,934 store sheep; 24,089 fat cattle; 60,722 fat sheep. The Maud Wednesday mart continued until 2002 when about 6,000 animals from across Scotland were sold. Following the closure of the mart the site was acquired by Maud Village Trust and has since been redeveloped for the benefit of the community with a housing project, attractive community gardens and a community service centre including medical and other facilities.

The extensive goods yards at the station have now been converted into a landscaped car park with attractive flowerbeds and picnic areas. The buildings on the island platform house the fascinating Maud Railway Museum and a few small business units. The Museum contains a cornucopia of artefacts relating to the Great North of Scotland Railway; open during several weekends in the summer, it is staffed by knowledgeable and enthusiastic volunteers.

A Second World War pill box is sited on the embankment just outside Maud station. It overlooks the road junction and is close to a pedestrian underpass.

The Buchan Combination Poorhouse, which later became Maud Hospital, was sited in Maud because it was easily accessible by rail from across Buchan.

Auchnagatt Public Hall was moved to the village from Stuartfield where it originated as the East Independent Church.

Walking the Line : Maud to Dyce

Maud Hospital (Buchan Combination Poorhouse) (NJ 925 476): Originally the Buchan Combination Poorhouse, this imposing institution opened on 26 January 1869, having taken three years to build. It housed 150 inmates including *'ordinary paupers, desolate women and lunatic poor'*, initially from the 16 parishes which had contributed towards the venture. By 1881, 26 parishes spread across Buchan were involved, with beds for the inmates allocated to each parish according to the size of its contribution. The 'New Maud' site was chosen because it was central to the district and easily reached by rail. The presence of the poorhouse increased the school roll, boosted trade for bakers who supplied bread, tailors who made tweed or corduroy suits for the inmates, and the craftsmen required to maintain the building and even to provide coffins and arrange funerals.

The poorhouse was overseen by a married Governor whose wife was expected to serve as matron. Staff turnover was high, reflecting the low rate of pay. At first conditions were extremely spartan, inmates slept on hair mattresses and floors were bare boards. It was deliberate policy to ensure that life in the poorhouse was *'more irksome than labour in order to discourage the idle poor'*. However, conditions gradually improved, partly due to the generosity of locals who gifted comforts, and by 1873 country walks and summer outings to Strichen Woods, Aden and Pitfour were arranged for the inmates. Male inmates were set to work in the farmland round the poorhouse, laboriously digging the 12 acres of land by hand. Oats and vegetables were grown and pigs and cows were raised, enabling the poorhouse to be largely self-sufficient and to have some surplus produce to sell. Women were expected to sew, knit and do domestic work.

In 1930 the institution was taken over by Aberdeen County Council and became known as Maud Home. At this time it catered for 160 including *'ordinary poor, mental defectives, harmless lunatics and chronic sick'*. The building was gloomily described as having *'narrow dark central corridors, with dayrooms and dormitories on either side, enjoying neither cross light nor cross ventilation'*. The home was taken over by the National Health Service in 1948 and became known as Maud Hospital. It closed in 2008.

Den of Old Maud (NJ 917 469): 'Old Maud' is probably derived from the Gaelic *Alt* meaning a stream and *Mad*, meeting place. According to tradition there was a castle, a residence of the Earl Marischal, in this vicinity though no evidence remains. During the digging out of the railway cutting through the den the wide foundations of a building were disturbed and a few coins were found. This may have been the Manor Place of Old Maud, a 17th century manor house built on the site of an earlier motte.

Auchnagatt (NJ 931 418): The name Auchnagatt means field of willows, great numbers of which grew bedside the Ebrie and were woven into the baskets and creels, often used as donkey paniers, for which the village was famed. The Baron's Inn, established before 1858, situated at the junction of minor roads with the coach road from Aberdeen, was a rest place for stage coach passengers and a staging post for changing horses. The station, affectionately known as 'The Gatt', had sidings and several goods sheds and was surrounded by a cluster of shops, including a bank and saddlers. You can still see the platform edges and the gate to the goods yard. One shop, an extraordinary emporium selling a diverse range of goods, remains at the time of writing.

Auchnagatt Public Hall, an attractive stone clad, cream washed building sited adjacent to the Line close to the site of the station, has an unusual history, having originated in Stuartfield as the East Independent Church. This short lived Church was formed in 1892 under the leadership of the Rev George Johnston, ex-minister of the Church of Deer. The wooden building stood at the bottom of Mill Street in Stuartfield until its demise as a church in 1906.

Looking south over the Line from Burngrains Bridge.

At that time a committee in Auchnagatt decided that the village needed a public hall and the community raised sufficient funds to purchase the building and relocate it to the village.

Burngrains, (NJ 936 400): During the early part of the 19th century a merchant from Clochcan ran a shop at Burngrains every Tuesday. He dealt in an astonishingly wide range of commodities, exchanging local farm produce *'butter, cheese, eggs, calves, swine, grain, honey etc'* for *'a miscellaneous assortment of goods, besides groceries ropes, tar, sweeties, oil, candles, lamps, lanterns, dishes of all sorts, combs, needles, thread, worsted, all sorts of cloth worn in the country, mittens, pots marbles, pigs, mousetraps, cutlery, bones for manure, guano, coats etc...as his trade was extensive and his profits extraordinary he was at this time very rich.'* (William Presslie).

Savoch Church

The War Memorial on the lower terrace of Savoch kirkyard overlooks gently rolling countryside from which many of those whom it commemorates must have originated.

Savoch Church (NJ 931 401): Isolated Savoch Church, a plain rectangular building with a birdcage belfry over the gable, was built in 1834, the cost being raised from public donations and the architect reputedly receiving 'a snuff box for his trouble'. As an obelisk in the upper terrace of the tranquil kirkyard states, '*this churchyard laid out by the parishioners at a cost of £300 was opened in 1877*'. The lower terrace contains excellent Victorian gravestones and a further elegant pink granite obelisk, the parish war memorial, recording 39 deaths in the First World War and four from the Second. The church closed in October 1997.

Arnage Station (NJ 932 361): On 12 March 1874 a muddle over the use of the passing loop at Arnage and misdirected signalling caused the first head-on collision on a single line section of the GNSR, at Gallowhill, just south of the station. This collision between a light engine running south and a mixed train heading for Peterhead, both of which were running late, resulted in the deaths of three footplate staff and the severe injury of a fourth.

The platform is now pleasantly overgrown with saplings and wildflowers, periwinkles, primroses and honeysuckle, encroaching from the grounds of Arnage Castle.

Arnage Castle (NJ 934 369): Arnage Castle was built about 1650 by Thomas Leiper, a local master mason, probably on the site of an earlier building. Originally a Z-plan castle, it was greatly altered in the 19th century when the first floor windows were enlarged and an imposing baronial entrance was added. It was described by Pratt in 1858 as '*a castellated rather than a Gothic building, and, with a few judicious alterations in harmony with its original style would hold a prominent place among the houses of distinction in the neighbourhood*'. Provost John Ross of Aberdeen bought Arnage in 1702 and it remained with his family until 1937 when the estate was sold. Between 1775 and 1790 John Ross of Arnage was a plantation factor in East Florida; surviving historical estate papers include a claim against him for the granting of manumission (freedom) to a slave. From 1937 until his death in 1976, the castle was owned by the wealthy builder Donald Charles Stewart (D.C. Stewart). Stewart was a Rolls Royce and steam traction engine owning philanthropist with a penchant for antiques and entertaining the glitterati of screen and stage at lavish parties.

William Presslie was born in 1832 at the Porter's Lodge of Arnage Castle, close to the woods of Arnage about a mile away from the present South Lodge. William's early education was frequently interrupted by the need to work seasonally as a herd loon, looking after 'free range' cattle, but later, whilst he was employed at the House of Leask, home of John Gordon of Cairnbulg, William was given the freedom of the library. William's own determination and the support of the Gordon family enabled him to qualify firstly as a school teacher and later as an Episcopalian clergyman.

Honeysuckle, one of the many wildflowers gradually taking over the station platform at Arnage.

William's autobiography, *The Uncommon Herd*, reprinted in 2012, contains a fascinating picture of life in the area, lamenting the effect that the enclosure of land had on poor families: '*When I was a boy every farmer required one or two persons to keep his cattle: now wire and wooden palings, hawthorn and holly hedges, and stone and earthen fences perform the work formerly assigned to the herd boy. This was a serious loss to many poor people with large families especially in the country. Although they got but little wages for herding still their meat even was considered a great deal...it was an excellent thing for boys intended for farm servants...it seasoned them to endure cold and rainy weather.*'

William's grandmother lived close by at Burngrains and had a prodigious memory for the stories which she had heard in her childhood evenings, when '*no other light was used in country houses but a peat-fire, the whole household usually spent their long winter evenings in spinning wool and lint (flax), or in weaving (knitting) stockings for which employment little light was needed stories were told.*'

The ill-fated Hilton of Turner Hall windmill lost its sails in the great storm of 28 December 1879 which also caused the Tay Bridge disaster.

Gallowhill of Ellon (NJ 931 350): According to the Great North of Scotland Railway Guide of 1881, '*on the brow of the hill is a clump of trees, marking the spot where the gallows stood in the old days when lairds had the power of 'pit and gallows.'* The Ebrie is thought to have been used as 'the pit' for drownings.

Hilton of Turner Hall (NJ 941 341): All that remains of the ill-fated Hilton Windmill is the cylindrical stubby pink granite tower. Built in the late 18th century to power a threshing machine, the windmill lost its sails on 28 December 1879, during the storm which caused the Tay Bridge disaster. The windmill was then capped and an external three horse gin was used to power the threshing mill. Later this was replaced by a stationary engine in the base of the tower. This caught fire destroying the original timber work and fittings of the mill.

Turner Hall was so named by John Turner, a 17th century merchant trading with Danzig, who had the name of the district changed from Rosehill to immortalise his own name. The Turners were active Jacobites. After his support for the cause in 1745, John Turner was forced into hiding for several years. His mother, Margret Turner '*was most active in engaging men for her son and sent several after him to the Highlands*' (Tayler).

Auchtercraig (NJ 948 313): See photograph of Foresters Terrace below.

MacDonald Golf Course, Ellon (NJ 950 314): The golf course covers about 40 acres within McDonald Park which was gifted to the town of Ellon by Sir James Gordon McDonald, KCB. Born in 1867, the son of a factor of Ellon Castle, James McDonald was educated in Ellon and at Robert Gordon's College in Aberdeen. In 1890 he went to Rhodesia and was employed by Cecil Rhodes whose trusted friend he became. McDonald amassed great personal wealth through employment in various spheres including farming, ranching, estate management, finance and gold mining. McDonald also acted as confidential advisor to various local governors and government ministers and as a result was knighted in 1929. Following his retirement Sir

Foresters Terrace (NJ 948 306): The row of houses in the foreground was built by members of the Ancient Order of Foresters, a friendly society providing benefits and support to its members in times of adversity. Behind the terrace, set back from Commercial Road, the crenelated entrance tower and candle snuffer turrets of Auchtercrag can be seen. The house was built in 1894 for William Smith, owner of the nearby Boot and Shoe Factory, its most successful product was the tackety boots worn by farm workers.

James Gordon McDonald lived between Rhodesia and Ellon and had a wing, reserved for his exclusive use, built on to the Station Hotel. In 1919, when the Ellon Castle Estate was being broken up and sold off, McDonald bought part of the castle policies. Some of the land was used to build a retirement home for his parents, the rest became woodland, a park and the 40 acre golf course he subsequently gave to the people of Ellon. The 9 hole golf course was designed by Stewart Burns, a golf professional from Cruden Bay, and was officially opened on 1 June 1927. During the Second World War McDonald joined the Ellon Home Guard but also served as an intelligence officer, dying on 7 December 1942 when SS *Ceramic*, on which he was sailing to South Africa, was torpedoed by a German U-boat.

During the War part of the Golf Course was used to graze sheep and to grow food crops. However, concealed in a wooded area in the South West corner, there was also a secret underground installation thought to have been used as Ellon Auxiliary Unit Patrol Operational Base. This was probably the first of two patrol bases in the Ellon area to have been built early in the war before a larger base was constructed in Target Wood south of Ellon. Later the site was probably used by the Home Guard and as an arms dump. Prime targets for sabotage by the patrol members following an invasion would have included the road and rail bridges over the Ythan and the railway line itself. In 1978 the course was extended to 18 holes by the purchase of land from Auchterellon Farms. In 1995, following the sale of some land owned by the club for housing, a new purpose built Club House was opened, replacing the former facility in the maternity unit of the old Ellon Hospital.

Ellon (NJ 955 305): Ellon, thought to derive its name from the Gaelic, *Eilean*, an island, from the islands in the river Ythan, grew up round the ford which was the first safe crossing place upstream from the Ythan estuary – making Ellon the gateway to Buchan. As early as 400 BC there was a Pictish settlement here and it was from the motte and bailey castle on Moot Hill of Ellon, overlooking the ford that, in the Middle Ages, the Comyn Earls of Buchan dispensed justice. Part of the Jacobite Army, under the command of Lord George Murray, used the ford to cross the Ythan during its march north and was said to have received support from the town.

Until improvements in road transport made movement of goods by road more economical,

The wonderfully baronial Station Hotel at Ellon, built in 1891, overlooked the station and reflected Ellon's confident expansion to the west following the coming of the railway. After his retirement Sir James Gordon McDonald lived between Rhodesia and Ellon and had a wing built for his exclusive use at the hotel.

A southbound train calls at Ellon in the early twentieth century. The first vehicle is a meat van, while the wagon behind the third coach would have been carrying fish in barrels. Today you have to draw on your imagination to see where the station buildings were located. (GNSR Association)

cargo was transported upstream from the Ythan estuary to Ellon on barges, firstly propelled by men using poles or by sail, later by paddle tugs.

Before over-fishing and pollution destroyed their habitat, mussels found in the Ythan's deeper sandy pools were the source of exquisite pearls. The large 'Kellie' pearl, presented to James VI in 1620 and incorporated in the Scottish crown, is thought to have originated here.

The granting of burgh status to Ellon in 1707 enabled markets to be held and brought trade to the town which was part of the Ellon Castle Estate. Ellon Castle has had several incarnations. The 16th century castle, of which only the round tower and part of a wall remain, was built on the Hill of Ardgith the site of the earlier Fortalice of Ardgith, seat of the Kennedys. The castle, then owned by the Gordons, was ruinous by 1851 when much of the dismantled stone was used to build a new mansion house, also known as Ellon Castle, which was demolished in 1929. Sections of the 3½ metre high deer dyke which surrounded the castle park have survived. The 18th century gardens, considered to have been amongst the finest in Scotland, contain a sundial commemorating the 18th century murder by their tutor of two of the Laird's sons.

The three-arch bridge built over the Ythan in 1793 eased the problem of crossing the river for road traffic and led to further growth of the town. With the advent of turnpikes around 1800 stagecoaches brought trade to the town's New Inn where horses were changed and passengers rested. Ellon's location within easy travelling distance of Aberdeen led to further growth following the arrival of the railway and again after the oil boom.

Ellon Station (NJ 948 308): The siting of Ellon Station a little outside the town centre resulted in the main focus of the community moving westwards from the Square to its vicinity. Not only the hotel but also a tannery, two auction marts and the hospital were soon situated close to the station and rather grand dwellings, the summer residences of wealthy Aberdonians, appeared on Station Road. From 1897 until 1932 Ellon was the junction for the 15 mile long Boddam branch serving several small communities, the GNSR's prestigious Cruden Bay Hotel, and the far more mundane Cruden Bay Brick and Tile Works. Constructing the new junction involved modifying the station layout so that the southbound platform became an island platform. This is now a grassy garden for the block of flats built against the northbound platform whilst the former goods yard houses an industrial development. The square structure at the North end of the down platform was the base of a watertank.

The four-arch railway viaduct which carries the Way over the River Ythan at Ellon. There is also a footpath along the riverside here.   *(Keith Fenwick)*

Ellon Viaduct (NJ 948 303): The 60 km long River Ythan rises to the North West of Ellon at Wells of Ythan and reaches the North Sea at Newburgh where the wide estuary forms part of the Forvie Nature Reserve, an excellent habitat for many species including eider duck, terns and seals. In Ellon, riverside walks have been developed giving opportunities to glimpse the elusive otters which live in the river.

The viaduct originally had three arches; the laying of the keystone of the third and final arch by Charles Gordon of Esslemont took place with great ceremony on 2 October 1860. Unfortunately, the foundations on the south bank were built into unstable soft ground and the bridge collapsed before the line was open. This delayed the opening until a four arched replacement viaduct could be built. When a statutory Board of Trade inspection of the line was carried out on 10 and 11 July 1861 the centering had only been removed for three weeks and there was already some evidence of subsidence. However, the new structure was approved and train services began on the line on 18 July 1861.

Esslemont Castle (NJ 932 297): The imposing, ruinous shell of Esslemont Castle is the second castle to have been built on this now overgrown site. Esslemont was held by the Marischal family from the 14th century; the earliest castle on this moated site, a massive L-shaped tower house, was destroyed by fire in 1493 probably during a feud between the Cheynes, who had acquired the castle by marriage, and the Hays. The present ruins are of the replacement, a three storey tower house with a round tower in the east corner, built around 1570–1590. Queen Mary stayed at Esslemont during her campaign against the Earl of Huntly. In 1625 the castle passed to the Errolls but was sold to the Gordons in 1728 and abandoned around 1769 when it was partially demolished and replaced by nearby Esslemont House.

Esslemont Station (NJ 933 289): Because this station was so isolated the station building, on the northbound platform, differed from the usual design by including accommodation for the agent. A disadvantage of living on the platform was said to be that that the house shook when a train passed through. Never profitable the station closed completely in 1952.

Bennachie (NJ 682 223): The prominent high granite tors of Bennachie, rising proudly over the surrounding lowlands are visible from much of the southern sections of the Formartine and Buchan Way. The distinctive rocky outcrop forming the summit of the Mither Tap (518m) is surrounded by the remains of an Iron Age hillfort. Later settlers on the hill included the

*Esslemont station
looking north.
    (Keith Fenwick)*

60 colonists who, by 1850 in desperation at the lack of ground available to them elsewhere, had dug out small crofts from the common ground on the eastern side of the hill. By 1859 the Lairds of nine surrounding estates succeeded in overturning the crofters' rights and forced them to pay rent or face evictions.

The Forestry Commission owns around 15,000 productive acres of woodland in the Bennachie area and maintains public access to the mountain through a visitor centre and a series of paths and trails.

*Bennachie stands out prominently
on the skyline to the west.*

The oddly shaped tower known as the Prop of Ythsie

Prop of Ythsie (NJ 884 314): Looking towards the northwest from the embankment between Monkshill and Logierieve on a clear day an oddly shaped tower may be seen in the distance, beyond Ellon; this is the Prop of Ythsie. This square red granite tower, a monument to George Hamilton Gordon, 4th Earl of Aberdeen, was built in 1861–2. George Hamilton Gordon was born in Edinburgh in 1784, and succeeded to the titles of Lord Haddo following his father's death in 1791 and Earl of Aberdeen following the death of his grandfather, 3rd Earl of Aberdeen in 1801. Hamilton Gordon, who sat in the Lords as a Tory peer, had an extremely successful political career culminating in his becoming Prime Minister in 1852. In March 1854 when the coalition government was divided over whether Britain should enter the Crimean War, Hamilton Gordon agreed, against his better judgement, to Britain's involvement. Reports of the bad management of the war and calls for an enquiry led to his resigning as Prime Minister on 29 January 1855. Hamilton Gordon, who was reputedly responsible for persuading Queen Victoria to buy Balmoral. died in London in 1860.

Logierieve Station (NJ 291 269): This station was originally called Newburgh Road as it was close to the Old Meldrum to Newburgh road. It was renamed after the nearby house of Logierieve shortly after opening. The name Logierieve derives from the Gaelic *lag*, meaning a low place and *reive* an enclosure for cattle. The station served a wide area stretching to Newburgh about 5 miles away to the east and including nearby

Logierieve Station, another one which is gradually reverting to the wild.

Pitmedden Estate.

Logierieve was a single platform station with a small goods yard which was controlled by a small signal box. The station house, which still displays a station clock, was for many years occupied by Willie Thompson, the Porter in Charge, who took immense pride in keeping the station and garden spick and span. He also had such a high reputation as a bone setter that passenger numbers at the station were increased by sufferers from assorted aches and pains arriving by train from far and wide to seek his advice.

Writing in 1865 William Anderson considered there to be nothing to be seen around Logierieve, *'but a house or two planted among acres of moss…a dull and barren prospect'*.

The railway greatly reduced the isolation of the area so that thirty years later Rev William Temple was able to state in *The Thanage of Fermertyn*, that *'Logierieve is situated on a rising ground overlooking what in days of old was called the 'Great Moss of Logierieve'. The prospect used to be very sombre, but now with the railway trains continually passing and repassing, its solitariness has been much relieved.'*

In the 17th century Logierieve, then known as Logieruiff, was the home of William Hay whose brother Francis was involved in a long drawn out and acrimonious quarrel with his former friend, Adam Gordon of Gight. Alas, the quarrel culminated in Adam being shot in the back by the riled Hay. Gordon of Gight, brother of Adam, then took matters into his own hands, rode to Logieruiff and, quite illegally seized Francis Hay and imprisoned him in his own lodgings in Aberdeen's Gallowgate. Forty-eight hours later Hay was brought before the Sheriff Depute of Aberdeen, a Gordon clansman. In this highly irregular trial Hay was unrepresented, death threats having been made to an advocate who offered to act for him. As a result Hay was condemned to be beheaded and next day, *'was led to a solitary spot and butchered by the swords of his enemies'*. (William Temple, *The Thanage of Fermertyn*, Aberdeen 1894.)

During the 19th century a Dame's School was situated in a cottage close to the railway station. For over four decades pupils were taught by Jane Montgomery who died in 1846 aged 82. According to William Temple, *'Jane was a worthy woman, a very successful teacher, and, according to the times, a strict disciplinarian. Few that received the rudiments of their education under her will forget her tall figure, her sand-glass, and her terrible tawse!'*

This road overbridge is just north of Udny station which can be seen in the distance.

UDNY STATION WITH THE 2.30 TRAIN.

Postcards of railway stations were once very common. This one of Udny dates from the early 20th century and shows a southbound train entering. There are several fish wagons in front of the coaches.

Udny Station (NJ 907 242): Yet another isolated station, situated on the boundary between the parishes of Udny and Foveran, Udny Station is an excellent example of an eponymous community which grew up around a railway station which then became its hub. The station also served the villages of Udny Green, Pitmedden, Tarves and Methlick as well as several extensive sporting and agricultural estates.

Udny was never a busy passenger station. The most regular passengers were children going to school in Ellon, but occasional excitement was caused by visiting celebrities, performers in concerts at nearby Haddo House. During the 1950s weekly ticket sales seldom exceeded £10 and as at so many rural stations the thriving parcel and goods traffic was the mainstay. 'Parcels' included an enormous variety of items; crates of dead poultry dispatched to London and Manchester by local dealers, seasonal game from the Haddo Estate, incoming live day old chicks, racing pigeons for release, calves in sacks, pigs in crates and a plethora of parts for agricultural implements. On a far less bulky scale were the many 'clubbie book' orders for local housewives. Udny handled up to 12,000 tons of goods traffic per annum including vast quantities of seed potatoes sent from nearby estates, including Pitmedden, to East Anglia. Surplus potatoes, destined for use as pig food so sprayed with blue dye to make them unfit for human consumption, also passed through the station. The presence of the station enabled consignments of draff from the Speyside distilleries and animal feed to be delivered quickly and easily to the adjacent Bibby's store for collection by local farmers.

An attractive floral display at Udny station. (Mike Cooper)

Udny Station Village (NJ 907 244): By the early part of 20th century a community had grown up in the area around the station which included the Station Hotel (at first owned by the railway company but later sold off), Bibby's agricultural store, a general merchant, North of Scotland Bank, telephone exchange, Post Office, garage and doctor. During the Second World War a barn like structure known as the 'Black Shed' was erected by the station. This was used as a strategic food store and had its contents regularly replaced until the end of rationing in the early 1950s.

The village benefitted greatly from the generosity of a wealthy local landowner, James Rollo Duncan. Duncan rose from very humble beginnings as the illegitimate son of a New Leeds farm servant to amass great wealth as a result of his expertise in mineral mining in Bolivia. Duncan built Tillycorthie House, south of Udny Station, where he lived until his death in 1938. Many of his estate workers were accommodated in houses which he built in Woodside Terrace and Duncan Terrace using granite brought by rail from the quarries at Stirling Hill (Boddam). Thanks to the setting up of the Duncan Electricity Company, Udny Station became the first village in North East Scotland to be lit by electricity. Udny Station Hall was provided for the community by Duncan in 1915.

Corthymuir Farm (NJ 895 237): On the night of 1 August 1940 the grain store at Corthymuir Farm was set alight by an incendiary bomb, one of twenty dropped by enemy aircraft. A further fourteen High Explosive bombs were dropped in a line running between the farm and a clump of trees close to the railway line at Tillycorthie Mansion House. This attack was probably intended for the decoy airfield at Easter Craigie, about 5 miles to the north east of the strategically important RAF Dyce. Decoy airfields were mock ups intended to deflect German air raids from operational airfields. Situated in poor agricultural land and equipped with false runway lights and enough troops to create the impression of activity they were indistinguishable from the real thing on German air reconnaissance photographs.

Tillycorthie Mansion House (NJ 907 233): Tillycorthie has the distinction of being one of the first concrete mansions to be built in Britain. It was constructed in 1911 for James Rollo Duncan. This extraordinary building combines vaguely Spanish and traditional Scots baronial features and was largely designed by Duncan himself. The house had a glass covered courtyard, large enough to allow the owner to turn his car in it and to accommodate a large granite fountain originally from the New Market in Aberdeen. The grounds included an artificial lake, constructed from railway sleepers, a workshop with a rooftop skating rink and two baronial lodges. By the late 1960s Tillycorthie was used as an agricultural store but has since been restored.

The former Udny Station Hotel was at first owned by the railway company but was sold off and was privately run for many years before closing in 2014.

Tillyeve Crossing (NJ 902 228):
The level crossing at Tillyeve gave access over the Line to Linkshill. The Crossing Keeper's house is situated close to the west side of the Line. The nearby overgrown duck pond is a bomb crater, a relic of the autumn 1940 air raid. At the time of writing the crossing gates, in a remarkably good state of preservation, were still in position, open to allow traffic to pass. From Tillyeve the Line began the 1 in 75 ascent towards Newmachar, crossing the watershed of the catchment areas of the Ythan and Don in the process.

The crossing gates at Tillyeve are in a remarkably good state of repair. The red disc was visible to engine drivers when the gates were across the track and road drivers when the road was blocked. A red light was added at night.

The Hill of Strypes: Satan's Den (NJ 894 208): North of Newmachar the Line climbs to a height of 450ft as it crosses the Hill of Strypes by way of a cutting almost a mile long and in places almost 50 metres deep. This infamous cutting, known as Satan's Den, along with the shallower cutting to the south of Newmachar station and the long exposed curve of embankment approaching it, were notorious for being blocked by snow as this piece of doggerel from over a century ago records:

> 'The Buchan train has gaen a stacher,
> She's got snoored up aboot New Machar
> May she be spared to rin more swacher
> In Nineteen hunder and seeven,'

During the blizzard of 19 January 1960 the second morning train from Fraserburgh and Peterhead became stuck in a drift 2½ metres deep. Despite heroic efforts of the railway staff it

South end of Satan's Den

Newmachar station looking north.

was almost 24 hours before the 57 passengers could be rescued by a relief train. Fifty soldiers from the Gordon Barracks, along with railway workers from as far away as Montrose, were deployed to help dig the stranded train out of the drift.

Newmachar Station (NJ 889 203): The station was situated about half a mile from the village which it served. The Station House, on the downside, was bought from a local G.P.

Newmachar had a smaller goods yard than many comparable stations. This was because since Aberdeen was within a day's journey by horse and cart it was already easy to move smaller commodities to and from the city by road so that the railway had less impact here than on more isolated communities. However, goods from further afield and bulky materials, such as those used for building Kingseat Hospital, farm fertilisers and draff were imported by train and it became easier to move outgoing farm produce such as grain, cattle and milk by rail. The station acted as a focal point for the daily distribution of newspapers to shops in Newmachar and neighbouring villages such as Whiterashes – a newspaper delivery boy had the unenviable daily job of cycling to the station to meet the first morning train from Aberdeen to collect a bundle of papers.

Newton Rubbing Stone (NJ 890 199): Set on the crest of the hillside to the north of the track, and looking tantalisingly like a Pictish symbol stone is a metre high stone pillar. Despite appearing on the 2nd edition of the OS 6-inch map (1901) and being considered important enough for inclusion in the RCAHMS data base this stone is a disappointingly prosaic rubbing post for cattle.

Newmachar Village (NJ 885 196): The village of Newmachar, formerly known as Summerhill, is central to the parish of New Machar which was created in 1609 out of a district previously known as Monykebbock, from within a larger, existing parish centred on the Cathedral of St Machar. The cathedral was supposedly named for St Machar, a follower of St Columba, who sent him as a missionary to North East Scotland. Machar is said to have founded a church dedicated to St Colms or Combs, both alternative names for St Columba, in what is now Newmachar. An alternative theory suggests that '*machar*' is derived from the Gaelic '*machair*' meaning flat ground near the water.

The new parish was known by a variety of names, chiefly variants of the saint's name until New Machar became that of the parish which has the village of Summerhill at its centre. Although the railway station, built in 1862, was always known as Newmachar the use of

Sleepers were erected by the side of the line near Newmachar for protection against snow drifts. Originally there would have been a continuous row of them but in this case several have disappeared.

Summerhill for the village persisted until 1908 when the Post Office began officially to use Newmachar – probably to avoid confusion with Summerhill in Aberdeen. Several gravestones in the kirkyard refer to Summerhill.

In 1639 a church was built very close to the present parish church and this, together with the adjacent parish school, became the hub of the community. The church was situated close to the centre of the parish on relatively dry land which was least likely to become an impassable quagmire in wet weather and which was crossed by the chief routes through the parish from the Bridge of Don and to the east and west.

By the 1790s the 'back road', the present B997, was officially designated a post road and mail was carried along it three times a week. In 1839 Summerhill became an official receiving centre for mail and could boast a post office able to sort letters, so that those posted there were franked with a local post mark. Prior to the coming of the railway mail was brought from Aberdeen by a horse drawn gig which arrived by 6.30 each morning, uplifting outgoing mail at 1pm.

The village became a nucleus for trades and merchants serving the day to day needs of the surrounding farms and estates. The streams in the parish provided power for several mills where grain, chiefly oats, was ground into meal. Pinkie Mill, south of Newmachar and powered by the Pinkie Burn, was the most important of the mills and remained functional as a meal mill until the early 20th century. The dam and sluice are still visible, although in the 1990s the dam was remodelled to provide a fish pond for anglers. In the 17th century there were at least ten handloom weavers in the village – by the 19th century this small scale cottage industry had been replaced by mechanised mills and factories. By 1837 cattle fairs were being held in Newmachar but were never on a large scale due to the proximity of larger well established marts in Aberdeen which had been sending cattle to Smithfield by steamship since 1820. According to the census of 1851, Newmachar could boast a shoemaker, no less than eight blacksmiths, reflecting the importance of horse power on surrounding farms, stocking knitters (this was a cottage industry), weavers, mill and wheel wrights, a grocer, a watch maker and surprisingly, a hat renovator. During the late 19th century the growth of Aberdeen provided a ready market for milk, increasing the prevalence of dairy farming. Dairying peaked in the 1950s when around twenty farms in the parish were involved. Newmachar is now largely a dormitory village for commuters to Aberdeen.

During the Second World War one of the highly secret Auxiliary Units, sometimes known as the British Resistance, set up to carry out acts of sabotage should invasion have taken place, was based at Newmachar. The unit, consisting of around six highly trained men, had both an Operational Base and Observation Post concealed below ground in the woods which form Straloch shelter belt. Had an invasion taken place probable targets for destruction would have been the railway line, including the bridges over the Don, the main road through Newmachar and the nearby airfield at Dyce, all of which would have greatly impeded the advance of invaders.

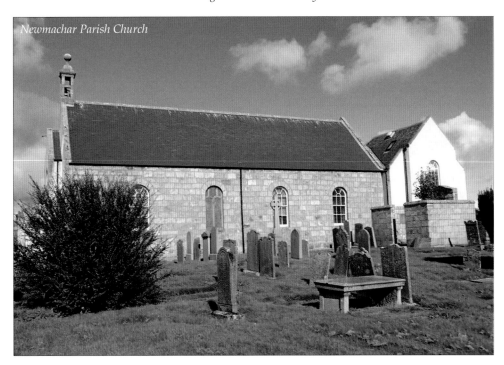
Newmachar Parish Church

Newmachar Parish Church (NJ 887 194): Newmachar church occupies a prominent position in the heart of the village and dates from 1791, when it replaced an earlier church of 1639. It was originally a plain rectangular building but is now greatly enlarged by a modern extension at the east end. The walls are of dressed granite, although all but the south wall are now harled. The west gable carries a birdcage bellcote, topped by a large ball finial – a clear landmark visible from the Line. A tall, narrow session house adjoins the church. The north and south walls both have four arched windows; these include the beautiful Crombie Memorial window, dating from 1915, and designed by Douglas Strachan, which illustrates St Machar and aspects of local history.

When Kingseat Hospital closed in 1995 the hospital War Memorial commemorating the lives of the five members of the hospital staff who fell in action in both World Wars was placed at the back of the church.

Thomas Ray, the hugely unpopular minister of Newmachar from 1729 until 1736, was deposed on 8 September 1736 on the grounds of his outrageous behaviour. Frustratingly, the only detail of the charge which survives is that '*he powdered his periwig on the Sabbath*'. Ray was found not guilty of this particular outrage but was deposed all the same. He was succeeded by Thomas Reid, minister from 1737 to 1752, who like Ray suffered hostility through having been imposed on the parish by its patrons Kings College, Aberdeen. The newly appointed Reid suffered the indignity of being ducked in a pond by his parishioners and needed an armed guard when he preached his first sermon but rapidly earned the affection and respect of his congregation. Reid, one of Scotland's greatest philosophers, left his ministry at Newmachar to become Professor of Philosophy at Kings College, later succeeding Adam Smith as Professor of Moral Philosophy at Glasgow University.

The walled Ramsay of Barra burial plot in the Kirkyard contains the grave of Susan Innes, widow of John Ramsay of Barra, and her second husband, Captain William Henry Nares RN. Captain Nares was father, by his first wife Elizabeth, of the eminent Arctic explorer, Admiral Sir George Strong Nares who was born in 1831 and during his boyhood spent considerable time at Straloch, a little to the north of Newmachar. After completing his education at the Naval College Portsmouth, George entered the navy and subsequently volunteered for Arctic exploration participating in an expedition searching for the missing Polar explorer Sir John Franklin. Nares had a distinguished career in scientific maritime exploration commanding both HMS *Challenger*, the first steam ship to cross the Antarctic Circle, and HMS *Newport*, the first ship to pass through the Suez Canal. Although the Arctic Expedition which Nares led in 1875-6 was unsuccessful in actually reaching the North Pole, he was honoured with a knighthood and Fellowship of the Royal Society. Geographical features including the Nares Strait, Nares Land in Greenland, the Nares Deep in the Atlantic and two Canadian Arctic Capes are named after him. Nares retired from active service in 1886 and died in 1915.

The burial plot of Wilson Argo and his wife Mary Bruce also commemorates their daughter, Isabella and her husband James Simpson, '*both suffered martyrdom in China during the Boxer Rising July 1900*'. The Boxers, were members of a Chinese secret society, the Yihequan ("Righteous and Harmonious Fists") who practiced boxing and physical exercises to make themselves invincible. The Simpsons were members of the China Inland Mission at a time when Missionary activities in China were regarded with great suspicion by many Chinese. Christian religious practices were deemed to be responsible for crop failures, flood, drought and unexplained deaths and the dilution of Chinese culture, politics, religion and technology. Hostility towards missionaries resulted in the Boxer Rebellion during which 58 missionaries and 21 children from the China Inland Mission were killed. The Simpsons were beheaded on 9 July 1900 in the Taiyuan Massacre in the Shanxi province of North China, one of the rebellion's most gruesome episodes.

Kingseat and Betterale Well (NJ 901 193): A track, reached by a footpath down from the Line, passes under the solum at NJ 898 192 to give access to Kingseat from Newmachar and leads to the modern housing development now occupying the site of the former Kingseat Hospital. Kingseat supposedly derives its name from Malcolm Canmore, King of Scotland, having rested there during his peregrinations in pursuit of Macbeth whom he eventually slaughtered at Lumphanan in 1053 AD. According to an apocryphal story Malcolm rested his army at what became known as Kingseat. The stone on which he sat to drink water from a nearby well was still being pointed out to visitors as late as 1894 and the name Kingseat appears on Robert Gordon's map of around 1637. The king decreed that the water he was given tasted 'better than ale' and henceforth the well was given the name '*Better Ale Well*'. According to the Canmore website Betterale Well was sited in a disused gravel quarry just outside the boundary wall of the Kingseat Hospital but is no longer visible.

Kingseat Hospital (NJ 904 190): Kingseat estate was bought by the Aberdeen Lunacy Board around 1895, at a time when a more enlightened approach to psychiatric care than that

Housing at Kingseat which replaced the hospital.

Aerial photograph showing wide sweep of the Line round Newmachar, necessary to accommodate the gradient. It also shows the commutation road and Kingseat development including the supposed site of Betterale Well. *(Cabro Aviation Ltd)*

which could be provided at Cornhill Hospital was gaining ground. The Board investigated the provision for psychiatric patients provided at the progressive Alt Scherbitz Asylum near Leipzig. There the emphasis was on a holistic approach to treating patients in pleasant surroundings where they could undertake meaningful physical outdoor activities. This became the model for the Kingseat development which originally catered '*solely for pauper lunatics belonging to the parish of Aberdeen City*'.

Between 1901 and 1926 ten villas were constructed in an attractively landscaped setting which provided an environment where patients could benefit from fresh air, a tranquil, spacious setting and suitable work on the land. This experimental concept, considered to be revolutionary at the time was beneficial not only to the 478 patients housed there by 1905, but also to the village of Newmachar. The excellent facilities for sports and recreation at the hospital were available to members of the wider community and the influx of medical, domestic and ancillary staff boosted the local economy. Eventually clinics such as baby care and chiropody were based at the hospital and were open to local people.

During the Second World War the Hospital was requisitioned by the Admiralty for use as a Navy Auxiliary Hospital and officially became HMS *Bacchante*, receiving patients from many incidents including the sinking of the *Royal Oak*. Naval patients also included the few survivors of the German attack on aircraft carrier HMS *Glorious* which, along with her escort of 2 destroyers *Acasta* and *Ardent*, was attacked by the German battleships *Scharnhorst* and *Gneisenau* whilst sailing from Norway to Scapa Flow in June 1940. The attack resulted in the loss of over 1500 crew and many aircraft. Some of the pitifully few (around 40) survivors who spent several days adrift on rafts in the North Sea were sent to Kingseat to recover.

Kingseat reverted to its role as a psychiatric hospital in 1946. By the latter part of the 20th century emphasis was being placed on care in the community resulting in a decline in the demand for places at Kingseat. The hospital closed in March 1995 since when most of the hospital buildings have been demolished to be replaced by a modern housing development.

Newmachar Cemetery (NJ 890 193): Opened in 1905, the cemetery on School Road contains 61 Commonwealth War Graves, most of which are of naval or merchant navy seamen who died

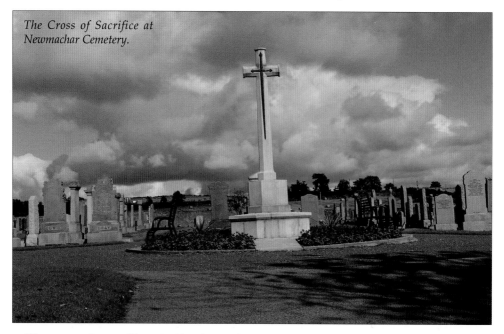

The Cross of Sacrifice at Newmachar Cemetery.

at Kingseat or the naval base in Aberdeen. Close to the entrance to the cemetery is the Cross of Sacrifice, designed in 1918 by Sir Reginald Blomfield, architect of the Menin Gate Memorial to the Missing in Ypres. This elegant white limestone cross is a feature of all cemeteries containing over 40 Commonwealth War Graves.

Standryford Road crossing (NJ 896 184): The unclassified road which crosses the Line by a bridge at Standryford is of interest in that during the 18th century this was the main route from Newmachar to the Bridge of Don and onwards into the city of Aberdeen. An example of a 'Commutation Road', it is a long established road with an interesting history. During the 17th century Acts of Parliament ordained that property owners were to pay 10/- per £100 value of their property annually for the construction, repair and maintenance of roads and bridges. Less wealthy individuals were expected to contribute around 6 days of physical labour as road builders. This particular burden could be avoided or commuted by paying 3d per day in lieu of work. The money raised by this was used to employ skilled road builders and the roads, including this one, they constructed were known as 'commutation roads'. The road appears on General Roy's map of 1747 – 1755 and as the main road on Taylor and Skinners route map of 1776. Because the road follows relatively high ground, avoiding the lower clay which turned roads into quagmires during wet weather, it was generally passable all year round and became the post road. The present A947, being a turnpike, was subject to tolls, making the commutation road a cheaper route into the city until the arrival of the railway caused the abolition of road tolls. As late as the 1930s this back road was being used by farmers to transport the daily milk supply into the city and also to walk cattle to the mart in King Street.

Elrick House (NJ 883 183): The estate of Elrick passed from the Hervey family to John Burnett in 1663, remaining within his family for many generations. The present Elrick House was built during the 1780s.

During the 18th century, whilst John Burnett (1748 – 1822) was serving the East India Company in Sumatra, it was leased to Sir William Fordyce, son of the Provost of Aberdeen. Fordyce was knighted for his skills as a fashionable London doctor and published several medical treatises including the splendidly titled, *The Great Importance and Proper Method of Cultivating and Curing Rhubarb in Britain for Medicinal Uses* first published in 1792 and now available as a digital edition.

The garden at Elrick contains a specimen of the beautiful white Fassfern Rose – the Jacobite Rose. In August 1745 when staying at Fassfern House on his way from Glenfinnan, Bonnie

Heading north towards Newmachar along the old 'commutation road' which linked the village with Aberdeen long before the later turnpike was constructed.

Prince Charlie picked a bloom from the rose and stuck it in his bonnet and it became the emblem of his supporters. The bush still flourishing at Elrick is said to have been brought there by Peter Burnett, 13th Laird of Elrick and to be a slip from a bush growing at the villa in Rome occupied by Bonnie Prince Charlie during his exile.

Signal box (NJ 893 189): On the west side of the track, a concrete plinth set into the embankment was the base of Elrick signal box which was built when the section of the line from there south to Parkhill was provided with double track to handle increased fish traffic in 1920. It was only used during the herring fishing season for 5 years.

In the 1950s, a gantry with six signal arms was erected here to test the sight of railway staff. The iron sockets in the embankment were the bases of the two signal posts. The base of the original signal box was a convenient location for the wooden hut housing the signal controls.

The curving downhill section of track from Newmachar to Parkhill, where speeds of almost 70 m.ph. could be reached, was one of the fastest stretches of track on the entire Buchan Line.

The signal arms used for sight testing at Elrick in the early 1960s. They would only be lowered when there were no trains on the line between Newmachar and Dyce. (Mike Stephen)

Parkhill Station (NJ 890 145): Parkhill Station has all but disappeared. It is marked by the remains of the single platform on the east side of the track and two tall stately evergreens growing close to the Line on the west side where once there was a small goods yard. The station, built to serve the Parkhill Estate and surrounding countryside, closed to passengers in 1950 although the goods yard survived until 1961.

Parkhill (NJ 900 140): Parkhill Estate, originally known as Glubsgoval, was the home of the Skene family from 1803 but was sold in 1920 to Dr James Crombie of the Crombie Mills who established the first seismological observatory in the North East at Parkhill.

In the late 19th century a heavy silver chain of a type worn by high status Picts was unearthed at Parkhill and is now preserved in the national Museum of Scotland. The chain consists of 23 pairs of rings and a terminal link, decorated with symbols of the type typically found on symbol stones, highlighted in red enamel.

Gavin Greig was born at Parkhill on 10 February 1856. The son of an Estate forester, Greig was distantly related on his mother's side to Robert Burns and on his father's side to Edvard Grieg. Gavin Greig spent his entire career as school master at Whitehill near New Deer. Greig is remembered for his colossal eight volume collection of over 3,000 folk songs and tunes, collected from throughout the North East. Many of the songs and tunes, including those of the Buchan bothy ballads, originated from all over the British Isles; many were very similar to Irish folk songs, reflecting the legacy of the Irish navvies who had worked on the construction of the railway. Greig's Doric play *Main's Wooin* was very popular before World War 2 and is still occasionally performed.

Parkhill Toll House (NJ 890 143): The Aberdeen to Banff turnpike followed the approximate line of the present A947. The railway crosses the road at NJ 889 145 by a replacement constructed during the formation of the Formartine and Buchan Way as the railway structure had been removed. Parkhill toll house is situated to the east of the railway line. For many years very dilapidated, this single storey harled building has a characteristic rounded corner facing the road. Work on this southerly section of the turnpike was delayed for seven years after the 1795 Aberdeenshire Turnpike Act until enough subscribers could be persuaded to finance the building of the expensive Don crossing. The first road bridge over the Don was built of timber and cost the then considerable sum of £2,000. It was replaced by the present stone bridge in 1851, but this has been much rebuilt since then.

Don Viaduct (NJ 888 142): The Line then crosses the river Don, the parish boundary between Newmachar and Dyce, on a three span viaduct 64 metres long.

The Don, at 63 miles the sixth longest river in Scotland, rises in the Cairngorms at Well of Don in Glen Avon and flows through the fertile farmland of the Garioch, receiving water from several tributaries including the Urie and Gadie before eventually passing under the historic Brig o' Balgownie and the modern bottleneck of the Bridge of Don to enter the sea at Aberdeen. Historically the Don was used to power industrial developments including both meal and textile mills. Textile manufacture included both linen and silk, established in the 18th century beyond Dyce at Stoneywood, and the cotton trade which employed over 4,000 workers by 1817. Tait's Papermill, established in 1852 at Inverurie on the site of an earlier meal mill, operated until 2009 producing specialist papers including the paper used for banknotes. The level of industry along the river caused pollution which had an adverse effect on wildlife. However, the water quality is again improving and the river now has good fish stocks, including salmon, eels, sea trout and brown trout providing food for its resident otters.

Beyond the Don crossing the Line loses its rural character on the approach to Dyce Station and although hawthorn, willows, sycamores and rowans line the path the noise of air

Orange hawkweed

The three arch viaduct over the River Don near Parkhill station, looking upstream.   (Keith Fenwick)

and heliport traffic increases as towering buildings and industrial developments come into view.

Mains of Dyce (NJ 889 138): The earlier mansion house on the site was the residence of the Skenes of Dyce until 1803 when, prompted by the building of the nearby bridge across the Don, they migrated over the river to Parkhill House. The house now on the site dates from around 1835.

In 1689 the Quaker Skenes had a granite mausoleum close to the mansion containing 16 coffin recesses built on a then wooded hillock, known as Howff Wood, now close to Cordyce School.

Dyce Village (NJ 890 130): The arrival of the Great North of Scotland Railway was responsible for the rapid growth of Dyce village on what had been a barren moor. The population of the parish in 1861 was 585, a decade later it had risen to 945. The majority of the feus in Dyce which became available in 1865 were granted to railwaymen employed by the Company. By 1867 a chemical works had been established and there was a granite quarry close by, along with a primary school and post office. The mission hall built on Victoria Street during the 1890s became the parish church in 1929. Two ponds near the station, which regularly froze in winter, were popular with curlers and skaters, including Aberdonians taking advantage of special evening excursion tickets to skate after work. During World War 1 a short lived camp for conscientious objectors was set up near Dyce granite quarry where the inmates were set to work breaking granite for road construction. Conditions were so harsh that the camp was closed in October 1916 after only two months. Until 1957, when the Greentrees Bar opened, Dyce was 'dry' and was known locally as the 'Holy City'

The establishment of both Lawson's bacon factory in 1934, employing 1300 workers at its peak in 1977, and Dyce airfield contributed to the pre-war growth of the community. From the 1960s the development of North Sea oil exploration and extraction accelerated both industrial and residential growth. Oil related activities brought expansion of the airport, the world's largest heliport, busy industrial estates and hotel developments, and completed the transformation of Dyce to a busy industrial suburb.

Dyce Airport (NJ 880 130): Dyce airfield originated as a privately run airport in 1934 when Eric Gandar Dower began commercial flights with the intentions of linking the Northern Isles

A surprisingly rural field near the airport which in May is thick with the delicate mauve blooms of lady's smock and studded with bright field buttercups and the occasional magenta spike of a marsh orchid.

with London and providing flights to Norway.

In 1937, Auxiliary Air Force Squadron 612 City of Aberdeen was formed from local volunteers who used Dyce to train as pilots and ground crew. By the outbreak of the Second World War they were flying regular coastal patrols from Dyce which became an RAF station in 1939. The grass runways became boggy with intensive use and were replaced with concrete in 1940; this enabled Dyce to be upgraded to a fighter station primarily carrying out convoy duties, U boat patrols and photo reconnaissance which led to the successful location and destruction of the *Tirpitz*. To reduce the possibility of enemy gliders landing at Dyce anti-invasion poles were erected on nearby farmland. The spire of Dyce Free Church was taken down during the war since it presented a hazard to aircraft.

During Operation Archery which took place in December 1941, fighter planes from Dyce carried out raids on German positions north of Bergen, this created the impression that an allied invasion of Norway was imminent. This subterfuge resulted in 30,000 German troops being diverted to defend Norway.

Looking south to Dyce airport over the industrial development, River Don and viaduct. The lake is in the grounds of Parkhill Estate.   *(Cabro Aviation Ltd)*

In May 1943 a German night fighter Junkers Ju 88 flying over the North Sea and defected to land at Dyce. This plane was equipped with Lichtenstein radar which enabled the Germans to detect the presence of enemy aircraft and was responsible for many RAF losses. This defection enabled the 'Windows' radar jamming device used by the RAF to be recalibrated to be effective against Lichtenstein and greatly reduced RAF losses in subsequent bombing raids.

The airport was nationalised in 1947 and transferred to British Airports Authority in 1975. Helicopter operations began in 1967 providing transport between shore and oil rigs; as oil exploration increased so did the importance of helicopter flights which now account for over half of all aircraft movements at Dyce.

Dyce Station (NJ 885 128): The Great North of Scotland mainline station at Dyce, built in 1854 close to Kirkton of Dyce, was relocated to its present site ¼ mile to the north to accommodate the Buchan Line when it became operational in 1861. The extended station was described as arguably the busiest station in the north and had four platforms – Buchan trains used the two easterly platforms. In the early days of the airport passengers arriving at Dyce station just crossed the railway line by the footbridge and walked to the air terminal, as did residents of 'dry' Dyce wishing to take refreshment in the airport bar. Although closed in 1968, the station reopened in 1984 and has been very successful, with a frequent service to Aberdeen and through trains to Edinburgh and Glasgow.

Dyce Station was the scene of an act of extraordinary heroism in May 1945 when a burning Wellington bomber crashed onto a goods train. Despite the horrific nature of the crash in which two crew members died and the inferno of flames and exploding bullets which engulfed the plane, 16 year old junior porter Morven Taylor pulled a trapped crewman from the wreckage, becoming the only railwayman in the North East to be awarded the LNER bravery medal.

The trackbed of the line as it approaches Dyce has been built over for industrial use but a route has been found for the Formartine and Buchan Way which ends rather unpromisingly at an inconspicuous signpost at the north end of the station carpark. The former Buchan Line building, for long a fish and chip shop, burned down in 2015. It is hard to envisage the glory days of steam when fish trains and cattle wagons from Buchan trundled through a bustling station.

In 1969, an excursion was run from Aberdeen to Peterhead and Fraserburgh on what was then just a freight railway. This is the return train at Dyce. The signal box still stands, as do the platforms on the main line to the left. But the Buchan line trackbed is now the car park. The footbridge has been replaced by a new one at the north end of the station. (Mike Mitchell/GNSRA)

A train from Peterhead approaching Maud in the early 1950s. At Maud, the coaches would be combined with the train from Fraserburgh. By that time, not many passengers travelled on the Peterhead branch but there was a considerable traffic in parcels and small items. This extended to livestock such as chicks in boxes and calves in sacks. The life of a railway guard was indeed varied.   (Sandy Murdoch)

Between Maud and Deer Abbey, the South Ugie Water meanders alongside the Line and passes under it several times. The banks of purple flowers are rosebay willow herb, also known as fireweed. In the days of steam trains the occasional lineside fire created ideal conditions for the rapid spread of the weed.

Walking the Line : Maud to Peterhead

The first dozen miles of this stretch of the Line largely follow the tranquil meanderings of the South Ugie Water and pass through gentle countryside which has been described as the 'Garden of Buchan'. However, from the Howe O' Buchan crossing towards Peterhead the Line deteriorates to become an urban footpath overshadowed by Peterhead's westward expansion. Although pleasantly landscaped, bright with springtime daffodils and planted with alders, sycamores and the occasional horse chestnut, little can be seen beyond the surrounding buildings. The path ends ignominiously on a large carpark behind Peterhead Academy and Community Centre, the one concession to its former status as a railway line being the bollards made of wooden sleepers at the crossing with York Street.

Aikey Brae (NJ 961 478): Aikey Brae means the oak covered hill. The wooded Aikey Brae is chiefly remembered as the site of the long established Aikey Fair, once the highlight of the rural Buchan calendar. During the 19th century Aikey was the largest horse fair in the North of Scotland, attracting vast numbers of horses. It was traditionally held on the first Wednesday after July 19, the feast day of St Drostan.

The exact origins of the fair are debatable. According to one theory it dates back to a celebration of Robert the Bruce's victory over the Comyns at the Battle of Aikey Brae which took place close to Bridgend in 1308, ending the devastating 'Harrying of Buchan'.

According to a further colourful local tradition Aikey Fair began when a travelling packman fell in to the Ugie, soaking all his wares. He spread them out to dry but before long passers-by spotted his goods and quickly made so many purchases that he promised to return to the same spot, on the same day the following year. More plausibly the fair is the continuation of a Lammas fair, established by an Act of 1661, which granted William, Earl Marischal, the right to hold an annual week long fair for the buying and selling of goods starting on the first Tuesday of July. The fair gradually expanded to become a major social event attracting firstly cattle traders but later horse traders and showmen. In 1926, on the Sunday preceding the fair when stalls were being set up, one showman started his merry-go-round and onlookers were quickly enjoying the ride. Thus began Aikey Sunday Fair which continued for several years after the demise of the horse fair.

During the early 19th century cattle sales were the main feature of the fair with up to an astonishing six thousand animals, including oxen used for winter ploughing, being sold. Before the arrival of the railway they were walked south from the sale to the huge tryst at Falkirk. Later beasts bypassed the fair and tryst, being sold at marts such as Maud which were close to stations, enabling them to be shipped directly south by train.

Horses, mainly locally bred Clydesdales, sold to buyers from across Britain then became the main part of the fair. After the sale they were walked in procession by locals to Maud station to be 'trucked' south. Each man would be responsible for a string of four or five horses, riding one and leading the rest, some of which were wild and unbroken. Frequently the Clydesdales were destined to be used to pull carts and wagons for haulage firms and carriers.

The widespread use of tractors and decline in the use of horse power in the 1950s sounded the death knell of the Aikey horse sale. The fortunes of Aikey Sunday Fair fluctuate and attempts to revive the event in recent years have met with mixed fortunes. The disused quarry site in which the fair was held is even being considered as a designated site for the Travellers who once flocked to Aikey Fair. There is a well preserved recumbent stone circle in the wood at the top of Aikey Brae.

Pilgrims Platform (NJ 966 480): During the 1930s, when the Abbey of Deer had recently reverted to the Roman Catholic Diocese of Aberdeen, pilgrimages to the Abbey were made. To facilitate these, what was the shortest platform on the line was built at the west of the nearby road bridge. At 9 feet square this wooden platform was so short that special instructions were issued for the excursion trains to

The platform at Abbey of Deer.   *(J L Stevenson)*

ensure that all passengers alighted from one door in the centre the train. The platform seems to have been in operation for pilgrims until around 1947, although no trace of it now remains. Pilgrimages on foot to the Abbey still take place regularly.

Abbey Bridge (NJ 966 481): This extraordinary bridge on the minor road linking the A950 and B9029 at Bridgend, about 50 metres west of Deer Abbey, crosses the South Ugie Water which here flows between the estates of Aden and Pitfour. The southern half of the bridge is narrower than the northern half; this bizarre arrangement arose because of a dispute between the Fergusons of Pitfour to the north and the Russells of Aden to the south of the river. The Fergusons' extensive landscaping of their estate included the creation of a 50 acre lake to which the Russells objected – claiming that it would cause flooding at Aden which lies at a lower level. The Fergusons ignored this objection and the lake went ahead. The Russells got their revenge when the Pitfour side of the bridge was widened to allow the Fergusons' superior new coach to pass oncoming vehicles on the bridge. The Russells stymied this plan simply by refusing to widen their side and so the uneven bridge remains passable for single file traffic only.

Uneven Abbey Bridge seen from the narrower south side. Half way over the Ugie the bridge abruptly widens as it passes over to the Pitfour Estate.

The ruins of Deer Abbey are now under the care of Historic Scotland and are open to the public during daylight hours, admission free.

Deer Abbey (NJ 969 481): The name Deer is an Anglicization of the Gaelic word doire, meaning the place of the oaks. The grey stone ruins of the Cistercian Abbey of St Mary of Deer are situated on what, at the time of building, would have been marshy ground between the shelter of Saplinbrae and the river. The proximity of the Abbey to the proposed route of the Line was one of the main reasons for Ferguson of Pitfour's early objections to the railway. Later he saw its benefits, including the financial gain to be made through compensation for the purchase of his land, and became a major supporter of the company.

The Abbey was founded in AD 1219 and fell into disuse after the Reformation, when William Keith, Earl Marischal of Scotland and Abbot and Commendator of Deer resigned his office in the face of criticism from the Church of Scotland. At any one time the Abbey housed no more than 17 monks who spent their days quietly in prayer, preaching the gospel, teaching and tending the sick and poor.

An earlier monastic settlement, the exact site of which is now lost, was founded by St Drostan somewhere in the vicinity and existed for about 500 years. According to the 9th century *Book of Deer*, St Drostan along with St Columba arrived in Aberdeenshire in about 580 AD and founded religious settlements at Aberdour and close to the South Ugie Water. When St Columba returned to Iona, Drostan remained as the first Abbot of Deer and together with his followers, continued spreading Christianity amongst the Picts. It was at this lost first Celtic Monastery of Deer that the incomparable illuminated manuscript, the *Book of Deer*, was written by the abbey monks. Now preserved in Cambridge University, the *Book of Deer* includes extracts from the four Gospels, part of the service for the visitation of the sick and the Apostles Creed. This 'official' content is in Latin but the monks added marginal notes forming a contemporary record of local events in what is now the earliest surviving example of written Scots Gaelic.

The later Cistercian Abbey site contained a cruciform church, cloisters and domestic buildings including the abbot's house, refectory, kitchen and dormitories. As their ruins indicate, they were all built from granite blocks with beautifully dressed stonework around the doors and windows. The church was aligned east to west and consisted of a nave, transepts and chancel. Following the Reformation, the Abbey buildings seem to have been used as a

When Deer Abbey was returned to the Roman Catholic Church during the 1930s the classical style mausoleum for Eliza Anne Ferguson, which was built on the site of the Abbey Church in 1851, was dismantled and the stone was used to build the Abbey entrance. Eliza Anne's grave is now marked by a flat gravestone.

quarry by anyone in the area who required building stone especially by the Fergusons of Pitfour within whose extensive estate the ruins lay. In 1851, Eliza Ann, the 21 year old daughter of George Ferguson, the 5th Laird of Pitfour, died and her distraught father constructed an ornate mausoleum on the site of the Abbey church. Quantities of stone were removed from the remaining Abbey walls and the ground level was lowered by about a metre, disturbing several much earlier burials in the process. The mausoleum, resembling a Greek temple and incongruous within the simplicity of the abbey ruins, was dismantled during the 1930s. Some of the columns and the portico were used to construct an imposing entrance to the Abbey site. Two of the now empty stone coffins which were unearthed during the building of the mausoleum were originally likely to have contained the remains of Abbey dignitaries and are still on display.

Pitfour Estate (NJ 977 487): At its zenith described as 'The Blenheim of Buchan' and encompassing over 50 square miles, Pitfour was one of the most extensive and grandest of the agricultural estates in North East Scotland. The estate originally consisted of 33,000 acres bought in 1700 by James Ferguson, advocate, who was to be the first of six Ferguson lairds. Much of the Ferguson fortune came from sugar plantations and estates on Trinidad and Tobago, including Castara on Tobago from which fine Caster sugar originated.

Successive Ferguson lairds sought to increase their prestige and social standing by adding to the ornamentation and amenities of the estate. The first three Ferguson lairds carried out ambitious but prudent improvements. They were sympathetic and progressive landlords, improving conditions for their tenants, and drivers of the agricultural improvement movement in Aberdeenshire. Later generations of the family made extravagant developments which consumed huge amounts of capital without increasing the earning capacity of the estate, so that the once great estate had to be sold off.

The extraordinary estate boasted a race course, an observatory, a canal leading towards the sea, follies and fountains, sunken gardens and shrubberies laid out in the style of Capability Brown. All this grandeur was in addition to a mansion house and several lesser houses, enormous stables and a private chapel.

The 50 acre artificial lake, said to have been inspired by Prince Regent's lake in Windsor Park, was dug in the early 19th century. Two bridges carry the driveway to the house over the lake and a smaller bridge crosses a burn flowing into the lake at the north east. The square Grecian design in the panels on the three arches of the north bridge, the grandest of the bridges, also occur on the stables and the extraordinary 'Temple of Theseus' which overlooks the lake.

The Temple, situated at the western end of the lake, was built after the lake had been dug out. This rectangular building measures about 8m by 16m and is a miniature version of the Temple of Hephaestus in Athens. There is great speculation as to the function of the Temple, varied theories include that it was for bathing, use as a boat house or for keeping alligators. The whole building is now very dilapidated but restoration work is in prospect. A boat pulled by a cable fixed across the lake provided a ferry to reach the Temple from the house.

Three mansion houses, each in turn known as Pitfour House and larger than its predecessor, were successively built on the estate. The final Pitfour House, built during the 19th century, was popularly said to have 365 windows, 52 rooms and 4 staircases, one for each of the seasons. The later addition of a portico along the front of the house had 12 pillars and continued the theme in the Greek style prevalent throughout the estate. It was demolished around 1926 when the estate was broken up; the stone was used to build Aberdeen council houses.

Behind the mansion house were the stables, and as one walks northwards through the estate the vast bulk of their derelict U-shaped block still looms through the trees. Built on the site of the home farm by Admiral Ferguson, the two storey stable building had provision for ten horses, four loose boxes, two coach houses and a harness room. On the first floor, above the stables there were six servants' bedrooms, there was also a coachman's house. The central carriage arch was surmounted by a wooden clock tower. The clock is still in place but the top portion and copper cupola which capped the tower currently lie amidst rubble in the yard.

A now vanished riding school, large enough to double up as a ballroom on occasions when the main reception room of Pitfour House was inadequate, was built a little to the north of the stables. In July 1894, the Buchan Agricultural Society held their annual cattle show at Pitfour with a bazaar in the riding school to raise funds for the new public hall in Fetterangus.

Curlers attending a Bonspiel on Pitfour Lake on Saturday 18 February 1888 travelled by train for the 3 minute journey from Mintlaw Station to the temporary platform erected by the Pitfour Curlers. Until the early part of the twentieth century curlers and skaters from the surrounding area often skated by lamplight at Pitfour.

The three arched North East Bridge carried the drive to Pitfour Mansion across the lake. The design on the rectangular panels was also used on the house and stable block and is in keeping with the Grecian theme of much of the estate ornamentation.

The ruins of the Old Parish Church at Old Deer.

The present owner of the estate is restoring the policies to their former glory and encourages responsible public access; a network of footpaths to link Aden Country Park, White Cow and Drinnie's Woods is being developed. Wildlife is being conserved and the lake, restocked with fish and used by a local fishing club, attracts large numbers of swans and wildfowl.

Old Deer (NJ 977 477): The first church at Deer was built prior to the Reformation as the 'mother' church for the parish when the Abbey was falling into decline. The church was built on a knoll on the bank of the Ugie in the probable vicinity of Drostan's first Abbey so that there has been a place of worship on virtually the same spot for almost 1500 years. A former Prior of the abbey, Gilbert Chisholm, became the first post Reformation minister of the parish soon after 1567.

The ruins of this church have pre-Reformation features such as doorways with fine mouldings and pointed arches and sculptured stones incorporated in the walls. It was in this church on 23 March 1711 that the 'The Rabbling of Deer' took place. The Presbyterian Rev. John Gordon was appointed by the Presbytery of Aberdeen to be inducted as minister of Deer following the death of his Episcopalian predecessor, Rev. George Keith. On the day of Gordon's intended induction a riot took place as the Episcopalian members of the congregation tried to prevent his entry to the church. Gates were locked, stones hurled from roof tops and muskets were fired into the air before the Presbyterians withdrew and the ordination took place elsewhere. The Episcopalians then forsook the village church for a meeting house built in the grounds of Aden Estate where their preferred candidate, Rev. William Livingstone, became minister. This Meeting House was burned down by Cumberland's troops in the aftermath of the Jacobite rising. According to Pratt, the wider repercussions of the Rabbling are said to have included the passing of the Acts of Toleration and Patronage.

It was also in the old parish church that, following his return from Culloden where he had served as chaplain to one of the Duke of Cumberland's regiments, the Presbyterian Rev. John Forbes felt it prudent to preach to his, largely Episcopalian and Jacobite supporting, congregation with his sword laid on the pulpit cushion. Despite this Rev. Forbes retained his pulpit at Deer until his death in 1769, by which time he had served the parish for half a century.

Part of the Bonnie Dundee window in St Drostan's Church.

Medieval relics set into the wall of the old parish kirk, Old Deer. It was here that the Rabbling of Deer took place in 1711.

By the 1780s this church was falling into disrepair and was inadequate for the large congregation drawn from the expanding villages of Mintlaw, Stuartfield and Fetterangus, all of which were within the Parish of Deer. The adjacent present parish church was completed as replacement in 1789. The conspicuous tower, almost 34 metres high, and the porch built from Aikey Brae granite were added in 1880 when the building was thoroughly renovated.

St Drostan's Episcopal Church (NJ 978 477): St Drostan's Episcopal Church was built in 1851, replacing an earlier, by then ruinous church on Chapel Green, only a short distance from the ruins of the old Parish Church, site of the infamous Rabbling of Deer. The land on Abbey Street on which the church was built along with many of the church furnishings, the stained glass east windows and the silver communion vessels were gifted by the Russells of Aden. In 1896 the chancel was extended in memory of Dean Arthur Ranken who died in 1889 having served the parish for 52 years.

Some of the bones of John Graham of Claverhouse, Viscount Dundee, (Bonnie Dundee or Bluidy Clavers, according to one's perspective) were buried in the chancel of St Drostan's having been gifted to Dean Ranken in 1852. A stained glass window in the south wall of the chancel is dedicated to Viscount Dundee who was shot whilst leading the Jacobite force at the Battle of Killiecrankie on 27 July 1698.

St Drostan's Episcopal Church, Old Deer. Deaconess Anna Ritchie is commemorated by a granite slab close to the church on the right of the porch.

Abbey Street, Old Deer. The Parish Church is straight ahead, with the trees of Aden Park behind it. St Drostan's Episcopal Church is set back from the road near the bus stop on the right.

Newlands (NJ 969 483): Newlands was originally the gardener's cottage for Pitfour Estate but was purchased in 1929 by Anna Ritchie for her parents, William and Elizabeth Park, who by then had retired from farming at Newlandhill, Strichen. Anna Ritchie was an extraordinary lady; born in 1884 she graduated from Edinburgh University before training as a teacher. Anna's life was beset by tragedy; her first marriage to Tom Smith was short lived, ending with his death from tuberculosis during the First World War. After some years teaching she returned to Buchan to look after her widowed mother and in December 1934 married Dr James Ritchie of Mavisbank, Old Deer, who tragically died the morning after their marriage. Later Anna was also involved in a serious, disfiguring car accident. These tragedies heightened her sympathy for the difficulties of others, especially of children with special needs, for whom little educational provision existed then. She spent one or two days a week travelling about the North East home-educating children with special needs. This culminated in her badgering Aberdeenshire Education Committee, of which she was a member for over thirty years, to establish the special needs school in Peterhead which was named in her honour. The Anna Ritchie School opened in 1963 and was later followed by Willowbank Day Care Centre for adults with special needs. From Newlands she established a postal Sunday school for children living in remote areas. In 1942 Anna Ritchie became the first Deaconess of the Scottish Episcopal Church and served at St Drostan's, Old Deer for many years. She was appointed MBE in recognition of her work. She died peacefully in her sleep in December 1971. A small granite plaque marks the resting place of her ashes outside the main door of St Drostan's Church.

Following Anna Ritchie's death, Newlands passed to her nephew, Arthur Kitchin, the distinguished Edinburgh cardiologist, who had spent time there as an evacuee during the Second World War. Dr Kitchin died on 15 May 2012.

Saplinbrae House (NJ 973 484); Now the main surviving property in the Pitfour Estate policies, Saplinbrae House was built in 1756. The Douglas firs behind the house were grown from Canadian seed which was sent to Scotland by Lord Pitfour's brother-in-law General James Murray. Taking its name from the wooded hill a little to the west of the house, Saplinbrae was first used as a coaching inn for travellers on the Banff to Peterhead road. However, by 1760 it had become the manse for the minister of the Qualified Episcopal Chapel which Lord Pitfour had built on the opposite side of the coach road.

When Admiral Ferguson's widowed mother-in-law, Lady Langford, moved north in the 1850s the house was altered to become the Dower House, unfortunately using stones plundered from Deer Abbey.

By 1877 the Fergusons were in financial difficulties and Saplinbrae was leased out for the annual rental of £40. It was later sold when the estate was broken up.

According to the *Buchan Observer*, early in the 20th century Saplinbrae House was described as, *'a secondary residence containing entrance hall, dining room, smoking room, ten bed and dressing rooms, five servants rooms, excellent offices and men-servants rooms in the garage'*.

In recent years Saplinbrae has been used as a country house hotel.

Old Deer Fever Hospital (NJ 976 482): For a brief period between 1884 and 1905, Meadowbank situated conveniently close to Mavisbank, traditionally the home of the Old Deer doctor, operated as a tiny isolation hospital chiefly admitting patients suffering from either scarlet or typhoid fever. The hospital had only three beds and was sometimes let out as summer lodgings but could become over crowded during epidemics, as on 31 December 1903 when there were seven patients. During 1897 there were 22 patients suffering from typhoid fever. The hospital became defunct when Strichen Isolation Hospital opened in 1905.

South Lodge, Pitfour (NJ 978 483): Although South Lodge was the main entrance to the Pitfour Estate it was constructed around 1850, about thirty years later than the West and Station (East) Lodges. Unlike the earlier lodges this is a two storey building and was probably two semi-detached houses before being altered around 1910.

The gateway is impressive, incorporating an imposing memorial to William Pitt, The Younger, and Henry Dundas, Viscount Melville, two close parliamentary friends of James Ferguson MP, 3rd Laird of Pitfour. The monument consists of two granite pillars topped by Grecian urns flanking the entrance at the ends of low, curving walls. A large stone panel on the east side of the entrance has a Latin inscription commemorating Pitt and Dundas. This translates as *'To the memory of William Pitt and Henry Dundas, Viscount Melville. Men of ancient virtue. This tribute, from the most durable native granite – than which their fame shall be more lasting – is given by James Ferguson of Pitfour, in the year of Salvation, 1816'*.

The main boundary wall of Pitfour is over 5 km long and in places 2 metres high. It was also built at the behest of James Ferguson MP, probably to give employment to his tenants during periods of hardship.

South Lodge, Pitfour

The imposing gateway to South Lodge, Pitfour, was constructed in 1816 as a tribute to William Pitt, The Younger, and Henry Dundas, Viscount Melville, both of whom had been close friends of James Ferguson during his time as an MP.

Cartelhaugh (NJ 979 484): Cartelhaugh, situated close to Pitfour South Lodge, was built soon after 1760 by James Ferguson, 3rd Laird of Pitfour, as a coaching inn to serve travellers on the coach road from Buchan to Banff when Saplinbrae, the original inn, became the manse for Waulkmill Chapel. The inn, known as the Dambrod Inn on account of stonework on the front of the building which resembles the squares on a dambrod (draughtboard), had fallen into disuse as a hostelry by 1873. There is a strong possibility that distinguished travellers who have stayed at the inn include Robert Burns. Burns records in his diary that, during a tour of the Highlands by coach in late August and September 1787, he spent the night at Old Deer on route from New Byth to Peterhead and the Bullers of Buchan.

Pitfour Observatory (NJ 973 499): The octagonal Observatory is 15 metres high and stands on a hill 121 metres above sea level, making it a prominent landmark. The top section of the tower is constructed of granite but the lower part is of brick with stone dressings and was only relatively recently painted white. Originally there was an internal wooden stairway with treads projecting from the wall, now replaced by a spiral metal stair case. The main gallery has a fireplace and eight windows which give superb views over the surrounding countryside. Admiral Ferguson's racecourse, 16m wide and as level as possible, began near Cairnorchies before running for about 3½km through White Cow Wood, Auchrynie, Cabra and Gaval. The Observatory would not have given a particularly good view of the track but the admiral claimed to have built it in order to reduce the distance he had to walk to watch the racing horses. During a severe storm in October 1900 lightning stuck the flagpole and caused an explosion which

Pitfour Observatory was built to enable the 5th Ferguson Laird of Pitfour to indulge his passion for horse racing by watching progress on his 3½km race track in comfort. The tower in Drinnie's Wood is open to the public and is sign posted from the A925

formed a huge cavity near the base of the tower, scattering debris including bricks and lime over a distance of about 30 metres. The Observatory has been restored and there is public access during daylight hours.

Taitswell (NJ 983 487): Taitswell was the Pitfour Estate factor's house and is situated close to the East Lodge. The most notable of the factors to live at Taitswell was James Mitchel who served the estate in a variety of capacities for forty-eight years from 1790 until his death in 1838. Mitchel served the Fergusons loyally and with great integrity, he was popular and respected not only on the estate but in the local community. When he died he left a considerable fortune, a substantial part of which was set aside to establish and finance girls' schools locally in Fetterangus, Rora, Mintlaw, Maud and in his home town of Banff. The remainder of his estate was to become an endowment for the benefit of old men and widows on the Pitfour Estate; known as the Mitchel Bequest it is still in existence. He is commemorated by the street named after him in Mintlaw.

Pitfour Chapel (NJ 982 491): The chapel, now a private house, was built in 1851 by George Ferguson, 5th Laird, who was embroiled in a quarrel with the Episcopal congregation over the repair or replacement of their existing chapel at Waulkmill. The Episcopalians consequently built St Drostan's in Old Deer on land made available to them by Mr Russell of Aden. In a fit of pique Ferguson built a private chapel, almost the same size as St Drostan's and with a conspicuous tower, on a hillock to the east of Pitfour House. It is said that on Sundays the estate workers and staff processed to the chapel followed by the Ferguson family, the choir dressed in surplices and finally the priest. Twenty years after it was built the chapel required extensive renovation and fell out of use around 1876, an expensive face saving folly.

Aden Estate (NJ 981 480): The Aden Estate was bought by Alexander Russell of Montcoffer in 1758 from James Ferguson of Kinmundy whose own estates included adjacent Pitfour on the opposite bank of the Ugie. Within Aden were the village of Old Deer and extensive farmland which Russell, an enthusiastic agricultural improver, set about developing. His improvements included planting the wooded areas originally intended to provide shelter throughout the estate which now form a very attractive feature of the area.

Further improvements involved enlarging the mansion and building the unique semi-circular steading, coach house and gate lodges. Kininmonth and Ludquharn were added to the estate which at its most extensive covered 31 square miles.

The decline of the estate set in after World War 1 when maintenance costs rose and farm income declined. About 75% of the estate was gradually sold off but it proved impossible to

Pitfour Chapel is now a private house.

The ruins of the mansion house in Aden Country Park. The park is signposted from the Line at the crossing with the A950 near Pitfour.

make ends meet, forcing Sidney Russell, the last Laird, to sell Aden House and its policies, the remaining 52 farms and much of Old Deer in 1937. Sadly the estate, which was then used for shooting, rapidly fell into disrepair and the mansion became derelict.

In 1975 Banff and Buchan Council acquired Aden and began to restore the buildings and grounds and established Aden Country Park and Heritage Centre.

The well managed and attractive country park now covers 230 acres and contains several visitor facilities, including Aberdeenshire's Farming Museum, camping and caravan sites, a lake, Victorian arboretum and a sensory garden. Throughout the park there are extensive waymarked walks. The wooded areas contain remains of several Bronze Age hut circles, evidence of the earliest settlements in the area.

The unique semi-circular farm steading, dating from around 1800, and the slightly later coach house have been restored and currently house the museum, a café and a gift shop. The remaining outside walls of the Russell's mansion have been consolidated and stabilised, an indication of the lifestyle of the former lairds being given by the size of the ruins and the nearby laundry, icehouse and gasworks.

The unique semi-circular farm steading at Aden now houses a range of visitor facilities.

Mintlaw station in 1995, before it was damaged by fire.
(Hamish Stevenson)

Mintlaw Station (NJ 990 485): Mintlaw Station was for a while the terminus on the Formartine & Buchan Railway Company's line to Peterhead from Dyce. When it opened in July 1861 the station was temporarily known as Old Deer and Mintlaw, reflecting its position on the Fraserburgh turnpike, midway between the two communities. It was more convenient for the estates of Aden and Pitfour than for the two villages. The station was renamed Mintlaw in 1867, by which time it had a large goods yard and the line had been extended to Peterhead.

The cluster of houses and commercial premises which grew up by the station became known as Mintlaw Station and included J C Rennie and Co, Woollen Manufacturers. There are still several thriving business premises in the vicinity of the station.

A brick cairn on the trackbed at the west end of Mintlaw Station, unveiled by conservationist David Bellamy in 1987, commemorates the signing of the agreement between Grampian Regional Council and Buchan Countryside Group which facilitated the creation of the Formartine and Buchan Way

When this photograph of the goods yard at Mintlaw was taken in the early 1960s, coal was still a significant traffic, and it could be safely left on the ground. (Sandy Murdoch)

Station Hotel (NJ 991 485): This hotel has had several reincarnations; in 1862 it was the Buchan Railway Hotel, named for its proximity to the station, later becoming the Station Hotel, and then in the late 20th century it become the Country Park Hotel, for its proximity to Aden Country Park. When it was newly opened in 1862 the hotel, kept by Mr Davie, was described 'as comfortable and commodious'.

Mintlaw (NJ 000 483): Mintlaw village was established at the crossroads of the Aberdeen to Fraserburgh and Banff to Peterhead Turnpikes by James Ferguson MP around 1813, the year in which the Ellon to Fraserburgh stretch of turnpike was opened. The section of the Peterhead to Banff turnpike which runs through Mintlaw and towards which Ferguson, a County Turnpike Trustee, subscribed £300 had been completed in 1807. Stands of trees, predominately beeches, dating from this period still line the approaches to the village. The crossroads became the centre of the diamond shaped village 'square' which, as traffic has increased, has become an uncomfortable amalgam between a traditional village square surrounded by inns and shops with a War Memorial at its centre and a busy traffic island. The War Memorial, erected after the First World War, was originally positioned in front of the Pitfour Arms; its base is thought to have been removed from one of the many statues in the Pitfour Estate.

Mail and passenger coaches passed through Mintlaw several times daily. Its central position between Fraserburgh, Ellon, Peterhead and Banff made it a convenient place for passengers to be given a break from what was, by modern standards, an uncomfortable and slow journey. In South Street rest houses were available for passengers but by the 1840s these were superseded by the facilities of the Pitfour Arms Hotel in the Square. For a time this, the first inn to be built in the village, could claim to be the busiest in the parish. The remaining early 19th century traditional stone built houses indicate the cruciform layout of Ferguson's settlement. Cottages for the Pitfour estate workers, of whom over a hundred indoor and outdoor staff lived in the village around 1830, were built along South Street – creating a need for trades and merchants so that by 1841 the population had reached 240. The arrival of the railway in 1861 led to the building of substantial houses along the section of turnpike leading to the station, which became Station Road. However, by the 1880s, as the fortunes of the Fergusons declined, the village became less well maintained and the lairds began to sell off feus to offset their debts.

Mintlaw War Memorial, looking east with the Peterhead road in the distance.

The railway line skirted the northern edge of Mintlaw. Housing, commercial and industrial developments have spread from Mintlaw Station to the village. The Line passed under the main Fraserburgh to Ellon road; since the removal of the road bridge, it is necessary to cross this with care. The Happy Plant Garden and Gift Centre, one of the largest in the North East, where refreshments are available, is adjacent to the crossing point.

Auchtydonald (NJ 015 479): Now very successfully producing soft fruit, the farm of Auchtydonald has long been established; first appearing as Achidonalde as early as 1380, it later appears in a 1544 list of lands belonging to Deer Abbey. The early spellings which omit the T suggest that the name is derived from the Gaelic *'achaidh Dhomhnuill'*, Donald's field.

Thomas Cargill of Auchtydonald, a poet and Jacobite supporter in 1715, was accused of being *'disaffected to His Majesty and Government'*. However, in May 1716, he executed a bond pledging his loyalty to King George and was permitted *'to go about his lawful affairs'*.

Glen Ugie (NK 025 483): A short lived distillery operated at Glen Ugie between 1830 and 1845, when part of the premises were taken over by James MacKenzie, a Longside carpenter who established Glenugie Sawmills in part of the distillery. The *Howes o' Buchan* comments rather sanctimoniously, *'If everybody followed the example of the parishioners of Longside and converted their distilleries into sawmills, the world would be none the worse, we opine, for the transformation.'* There was a distillery of the same name operating sporadically in Peterhead from about 1832 until 1983.

Longside (NK 036 473): The land on which Longside was developed was originally part of the Keith estates which were forfeited in the aftermath of the 1715 Jacobite rising and bought by the York Building Company before being acquired by the Fergusons of Pitfour.

The small cluster of dwellings around the parish church became the nucleus of an expanding Longside around 1801 when 100 acres were set aside by the laird, George Ferguson of Pitfour and divided into crofts to be offered on leases of 57 years. These original feus led to the formation of the main street of the settlement which was laid out in a less regular pattern than the grid iron street plan of most other planned villages in Aberdeenshire. Arguably this irregularity adds to the charm of the village. The *Howes o' Buchan* describes Longside as *'perhaps the prettiest village of its size in the northern half of Buchan. Embowered in trees, it strikes the stranger as a sort of oasis in our district, generally so bare of wood....the village is entirely modern... having every wished for convenience within its own limits...merchants' shops of all kinds, a couple of pretty good inns.'*

By 1828 the population of Longside village was around 600 but as the fortunes of the Fergusons begun to decline so did the maintenance of Longside.

In 1827 James Bruce tenant of Middletown of Inverquhomery bought a huge tract of land which included the village of Longside from the Pitfour estate. The new laird was an efficient and considerate landlord, carrying out many improvements and treating his tenants with compassion. Successive Bruce lairds continued to contribute to the development of Longside, giving land to the community for the erection of public buildings such as the school. In 1886 a reduction of 10% in rent was given to all tenants, *'one of the many acts of kindness shown by Mr Bruce to his tenants and the interest taken in their welfare in these difficult times'*. Other improvements included the construction of a new path to the station, removal of dung heaps and peat stacks from close to the streets and improvements to the market stance, and in 1873, contributing towards the provision of a gravitational water supply to the village. Street lighting in the form of acetylene and oil lamps was introduced to the village in 1908 and replaced by electric lighting in 1928.

Eventually the estate was inherited by sixteen year old Vincent Bruce and the celebrations held when he came of age in 1909 reflect the esteem in which the family was held. Vincent was taken to a celebratory dinner in St John's Hall by his tenants who removed the horses from his carriage and pulled it themselves. Following the outbreak of war in 1914 Vincent joined the 15th Royal Scots Regiment, later receiving a commission and transferring to the 5th Gordon Highlanders and serving in France. Lieutenant Bruce was killed on the night of 25/26th March 1916 by a German mine which exploded in a trench near Neuville, St Vast. Although plots of land were gradually sold off, the estate continued to remain in the hands of the Bruce family until 1943 when it was purchased on behalf of J. Sainsbury Ltd.

The Longside district has produced, over the centuries, several renowned characters and 'lads of pairts'; some of these, Rev. John Skinner, Jamie Fleeman, John Imray and James Annand are commemorated by street names in the village

John Imray (1820-1902), the son of Reverend John Imray, Parish Minister for Longside from 1820-1848 and his wife Catherine, had an illustrious career as an engineer. He was involved in several prestigious projects including the ventilation systems for the new Houses of Parliament and the Royal Yacht, preparing the ventilation of Buckingham Palace for balls, the repair of Lambeth Suspension Bridge and the design of St Pancras Station.

Annand Crescent commemorates James Annand (1843-1906), the son of a blacksmith at Kinmundy. He received his early education at Lenabo Dame School then at Longside Parish School. He became a journalist then, in January 1906, was elected as MP for East Aberdeenshire but died just 16 days later making him one of the shortest serving MPs in history.

Rev. John Skinner (1721 – 1807) became Episcopalian parson of Longside in 1742 and had a ministry lasting for an astonishing 65 years. In the aftermath of the Jacobite defeat in 1746 there was little tolerance of Episcopacy, forcing Skinner to disguise himself as a miller to avoid capture by government troops. On the night of 29 July 1746 his parsonage was raided by troops who set fire to the Episcopal chapels in both Longside and Old Deer. The Penal Act of 1746 forbade Episcopalian clergy from preaching to more than members of their own household and four other people. In defiance of this restriction Skinner continued his ministry by preaching from the window of his house at Linshart, the congregation sheltering between the two wings of the house. Consequently in May 1753 Skinner was imprisoned in Aberdeen for six months. A further offence would have resulted in banishment to the plantations. After his release a more circumspect Skinner was able to continue to live at Linshart but with a reduced income so that in 1758 he took on the farm of Mains of Ludquharn for seven years. Following the accession of George III, toleration of Episcopalians increased enabling Skinner to build a new chapel near Linshart which was first used for worship on 7 August 1763. Rev. John Skinner was highly accomplished and scholarly; he contributed to the 3rd edition of the Encyclopaedia Britannica and in 1788 published his two volume *Ecclesiastical History of Scotland*. Such was the esteem in which Rev. Skinner was held that, despite his earlier imprisonment in the Tolbooth, he was granted the freedom of Old Aberdeen in 1789.

Rev. John Skinner was also a much respected poet. One of his works, *Tullochgorum* was considered by Robert Burns to be 'the best Scotch song Scotland ever saw'. *Tullochgorum*, written at the suggestion of Mrs Montgomery, wife of the Inland Revenue Officer in Ellon, contains the lines:

> *May choicest blessings still attend*
> *Each honest-hearted open friend,*
> *An' calm an' quiet be his end,*
> *Be a' that's good before him!*

Rev. John Skinner met his own end on 16 June 1807 June and was buried at Longside with his wife Grisell Hunter who had died in 1799.

A cairn at Linshart marks the spot where, until it was blown down in 1953, a hawthorn tree known as the 'Tulochgorum Tree' grew, reputedly the place where Skinner wrote Tullochgorum and where members of his congregation sheltered to listen to his preaching. The song is also commemorated in a Longside street – Tullochgorum Gardens.

James Fleming's grave in Longside Churchyard is inscribed with the words 'Erected in 1861 to indicate the grave of Jamie Fleeman, in answer to his prayer, "Dinna bury me like a beast."'

James Fleming, affectionately known as Jamie Fleeman, The Laird of Udny's Fool, was born at Ludquharn and christened at Longside on 7 April 1713. He gained such notoriety as 'fool' to the Laird of Udny that a biography of him written by Rev. J Pratt was published in 1831, four decades after his death, and reprinted in 1980. Pratt explains that *'a century or two ago, a professed fool was considered a necessary appendage to every family of distinction. The primitive elements of his character were the knave, the idiot, the crazed madman. Wit combined with apparent stupidity, unbending fidelity mingled with reckless audacity, and a discriminating judgement concealed by a well dissembled indifference.'* Characteristics in a successful fool *'were part real and part feigned'*. Jamie was regarded with great affection for his ready wit, loyalty, discretion and trustworthiness, even being used by the Countess of Erroll as a go between, taking messages to and from the many fugitives, including Lord Pitsligo, who were hiding about the countryside in the terrible aftermath to Culloden. Despite his 'foolishness' Jamie could be relied upon, if interrogated, not to disclose the nature of his mission. When Jamie died in 1778, his last words were said to be, *'I'm a Christian, dinna bury me like a beast'*. Thanks to the generosity of the Kilgour family, owners of Longside woollen mill, Jamie got his wish and was buried with dignity in Longside kirkyard; weavers from their mill acted as bearers and they provided cakes and ale for the mourners. Jamie's grave was unmarked until 1861 when a visitor to the grave of Rev. John Skinner, having been told the story of Jamie's last wish, raised about £14 to pay for the granite pillar which now marks the grave.

Auchlee Bridge (NK 037 479): The first recorded Auchlee Bridge was constructed in August 1624 at the behest of the Kirk session when, according to the session minutes, the Minister went to Fraserburgh to buy thirteen trees in order to build the bridge and then arranged for the bridge to be constructed.

This wooden bridge was replaced by a single arched stone bridge bearing a 1742 date stone. The increased traffic generated by the arrival of the railway was too great for the narrow bridge which by 1864 was described as being, *'an obstruction to traffic as well as to the more timid pedestrians'*. To avoid the danger of being forced over the side of the bridge by an approaching horse and cart, cautious pedestrians took a 2 mile detour to Bridgend to reach the station from the village. The road between the village and the station was also prone to flooding, putting users in danger of being swept away when the river was in spate. In September 1894 an embankment was built along Station Road to reduce this danger. The bridge was widened on the east side in 1900 and a confident *Buchan Observer* report of October 1900 declared that *'the bridge as it now stands will be of service for generations to come.'* The bridge held until 1995 when it partially gave way and was reconstructed with three arches, incorporating the date stones from the bridge's previous incarnations.

Auchlee Bridge crosses the Ugie to link Longside village with the railway station.

Longside station looking east. Only the platform edges survive. The station building was where the houses now stand.
(Keith Fenwick)

Longside Station (NK 038 479): Work on constructing the Longside section of the railway was underway by August 1861 and involved around fifty navvies most of whom lodged in Longside. For about a year they worked simultaneously in four gangs on sections of line to Crookedneuk, Bridgend, Longside and Auchlee. Work was completed by June 1862, enabling Longside Station to open for traffic on 3 July 1862.

Winter snow storms frequently caused difficulties on this section of the Line. During the snowstorm of February 1897 all roads and railway lines in the area were blocked and squads of men were employed to clear the railway to enable supplies to get through to isolated communities. In January 1945 a passenger train was derailed at Longside during a severe snowstorm. That winter the snowfall was so heavy that for about two weeks road and rail transport was impossible, and Forces personnel and civilian passengers were taken between Aberdeen and Peterhead by drifter.

Goods traffic at Longside ended on 23 March 1964 but passenger services ran until May of the following year.

From the station yard a state owned branch line, constructed in 1918, ran across what is now Longside Golf Course to service the Admiralty Air Ship station at Lenabo.

Station Terrace (NK 037 480): Despite the rather prosaic name, Station Terrace was generally considered by the Victorians to be the most upmarket area of Longside. The superior houses were built shortly after the arrival of the railway in 1862. Close to the station they were convenient for wealthy professional occupants who travelled daily to Peterhead.

Longside Parish Church and Kirkyard (NK 037 472): Within Longside kirkyard are the present Parish Church dating from 1836 and the older, now roofless, church dating from 1620 which it replaced. When the old church was built it was designated as the 'ower Kirk of Peterugie', Peterugie being the old name for Peterhead. However, since the farm on which it was built was called Longside both the church and the village which grew up round it became known by this name.

The entrance to the old kirk is through a lych gate from which a sunken cobbled path leads across the kirkyard to the old kirk, now filled with graves. The lych gate dates from the same period as the old kirk and is one of the few built to provide protection for the coffin and mourners as they waited to be met by the minister.

The old kirk was a plain rectangular building with an unusual ornamental bellcote situated

Longside Parish Kirks

above the doorway in the west gable. The bellcote is embellished with the Sibbald arms and the initials A.S. Abraham Sibbald was the influential Minister of Old Deer who gave financial support to the building of the church. Also on the belfry are the Bruce arms, the initials GB and the name Mr Meason, thought to be the builder of the church. Ministers who served in this church included Rev. Thomas Kidd who had what must be one of the shortest ministries ever in Scotland; he was inducted to Longside on 14 May 1829 and died only 3 days later.

By the 1830s the original Parish Church had become inadequate for the growing congregation and in August 1836 it was replaced by the present church, designed by the Aberdeen architect, John Smith. This was rather disparagingly described in the *New Statistical Account of Scotland* by the then minister, Rev. John Imray, as being '*a plain building for about 1,000 sitters*'. However the church is considered by Charles McKean author of an *An Illustrated Architectural Guide to Banff and Buchan*, as being '*an impressive rectangular building with a Tudorish west gable capped by a bellcote*'. The burial ground, which was extended in 1872, contains several interesting graves including those of the Rev. John Skinner, Jamie Fleeman and an intricate Celtic cross commemorating William Rudolf Gentle, a naval surgeon who died when his ship HMS *Russell* was sunk in 1916.

St John's Episcopal Church (NK 040 471): St John's Episcopal Church replaced two earlier Episcopal Chapels. The earliest, at Linshart, was opened on 7 August 1763 and was in use until 1801 when it was replaced by a chapel built in the vicinity of the Parish Church. The

Lych gate at Longside.

first minister of the new chapel was Rev. John Cumming who had succeeded his grandfather Rev. John Skinner as incumbent. By the time of Rev. Cumming's death in 1849 he and his grandfather between them had been clergymen in Longside for over a century. No trace now remains of this second chapel which was replaced by St John's Church in 1854.

Built of stone from the nearby Cairngall quarries, St John's has a distinctive and conspicuous crow stepped central tower, about 30 metres tall, standing proud of the surrounding trees. The hall adjacent to the church was opened in 1888.

Inside the church, above the west door is an airship propeller, inscribed with the names of its crew. This is all that remains of HMA C25, one of the airships based at RNAS Longside, which was shot down over the sea close to Rattray Head on 31 July 1918.

Auchlee (NK 042 482): The current Auchlee Farmhouse was built in 1882 using stone from the by then long defunct Auchlee Woollen Mill. This mill, for many years a major source of employment in the district, produced high quality woollen cloth for the Peterhead woollen trade and was owned by the Kilgours of Kinmundy. The mill, built close to the bank of the Ugie in 1795, was an extension of the Kilgours' already well-established Kinmundy business. Water to power the mills was diverted from the Ugie to the enlarged Loch of Auchlee; dyeing sheds and houses for millworkers were built at Millbank. Unfortunately, a downturn in the woollen trade caused the bankruptcy of the Kilgours in 1828; the repercussions were felt throughout the district. According to *The Howes o' Buchan*, '*It was not the rich alone who suffered. Every cottar or labourer who had scraped together a few pounds put it into the hands of the Kilgours. Nowhere, in their opinion could it be so safe, not even 'in the bank'...A large amount of misery was caused by this failure throughout the district... assets, when realised only amounted to a dividend among the creditors of 2sh-10d per pound*'.

Peter Still, regarded by his admirers as being as great a poet as Robert Burns but by others as merely aping Burns's style, was born in Fraserburgh on 1 January 1814. He spent much of his short life at Millbank Cottages, Auchlee, and his two published volumes of poetry reflect his love for the countryside around his boyhood home. Born into a labourer's family, Still, like many of his contemporaries, was taken out of school at an early age to act as herd loon

Longside from the north. The railway ran just south of the houses at the bottom of the picture. The road to the village bisects the golf course. The village itself is in the distance, with the Parish Church at its centre.   *(Cabro Aviation Ltd)*

The golf course to the east of Longside station covers the course of the branch to RNAS Lenabo which crossed the burn near the bridge which is visible and then headed to the clump of trees in the distance on the right. *(Keith Fenwick)*

during the summer months, sporadically continuing his education in the winters. Suffering from profound deafness and chronic ill health, he struggled to support his family and died on 21 March 1848, by which time he was Tollkeeper at the Blackhouse Toll on the Fraserburgh to Peterhead turnpike. Still's greatest work was 'The Cottar's Sunday', a sequel to Burns' 'Cottar's Saturday Night'.

Golf Course (NK 040 479): Longside Golf Course opened in 1979 and was extended to 18 holes in 1996. The golf course and club house were both established after considerable local fundraising and were largely constructed by local volunteers. The course is bisected by Station Road and the meandering River Ugie and extends across what was previously boggy land between the village and the river.

Cairngall (NK 043 474): Cairngall House, surrounded by wooded policies overlooking Longside Golf course and on the edge of Longside village, was the centrepiece of the Cairngall Estate. In 1931, when it was purchased by James Rollo Duncan of Tillycorthie, the 900 acre estate included granite quarries, by then largely disused, a blacksmith's shop, meal mill, crofts, and property in the village of Longside. Duncan had risen from extremely humble beginnings in New Leeds to become a tin and silver magnate amassing a vast fortune largely from his mining interests in Bolivia. The title deeds of Cairngall were in the name of Duncan's wife, Isabella, whose father, grieve at Cairngall Home Farm, died there in 1881 as the result of falling through a hatch in the steading.

The name Cairngall is considered to be derived from the Gaelic *Carn-a-gail* – the cairn of strangers. The cairn at nearby Hillhead of Cairngall is thought to be the burial place of a group of invading Danes. Particularly in the years prior to the First World War, Cairngall Estate and the attractive countryside around it were very popular destinations for employees' picnics and works' outings from Peterhead.

High quality granite, prized for the degree of hardness, was mined at quarries on the estate between the eighteenth and the early twentieth centuries. Around 1818 Cairngall granite was selected by Robert Stephenson as the most suitable stone for the base of the Bell Rock lighthouse. The dark, close grained granite was subsequently used for a wide range of projects including lighthouse building, part of the Houses of Parliament, the base of the Duke of Wellington's statue in Glasgow, pillars in Covent Garden Market and the eight vast pillars at the front entrance to St George's Hall in Liverpool. Probably the most prestigious use of the granite was the 30 ton block destined for the double sarcophagus for Queen Victoria and Prince Albert in the Royal Mausoleum at Frogmore. This was said to be the largest flawless block of granite in existence and was the fourth block to be quarried for use at Frogmore, three previously quarried blocks having been rejected. The perfect block was trundled to Aberdeen on a bogie pulled by a dozen powerful Clydesdales before being hollowed out, dressed and polished, by which time its weight was reduced to 9 tons. Even so the cavity had to be hurriedly enlarged at Frogmore in February 1901 to enable Queen Victoria's vastly oversized coffin to be placed beside that of her beloved Albert.

The remains of the officers' mess at Lenabo, with the memorial plaque.

Strawberry Bank (NK 046 479): In 1861, when the line from Peterhead to Mintlaw was under construction, the Great North of Scotland Railway bought 6 acres of land on what is now Strawberry Bank but was then, more prosaically, Brick Croft, part of the Pitfour Estate. The land was used to extract sand and gravel to provide ballast for the railway. Land in the vicinity has since yielded thousands of tons of sand, gravel and aggregate before being returned to agricultural use.

RNAS Longside, 'Lenabo' (NK 026 437): During the First World War there was a direct rail link from Longside Station to RNAS Longside, the most northerly of Britain's airship bases. Sited on boggy land at Lenabo, by which name it was often known, much of the peat extracted by the thousands of Scots and Irish navvies involved in construction was used to power the vast numbers of steam scoops, steam lorries, bucket cranes and locomotives used whilst building the base.

The railway spur, used exclusively for the base, was built in order to transport materials efficiently from Longside Station. The line ceased to operate in 1920, by which time over 32,000 tons of materials and stores had been carried by train to Lenabo. The track left Longside station yard and ran on an embankment across the haughs of Auchlee, now part of Longside Golf course, and crossed the Ugie near Strawberry Bank before running through Cairngall, Tiffery and Kinmundy to Lenabo.

The Airship Station became operational in 1916 when the first two (deflated) airships were transported there by rail. By 1918 Lenabo was the base for 12 airships and was designated an RAF station. Intended to provide allied shipping with additional protection from German U-boats operating in the North Sea, Lenabo housed three large airship sheds each 30 metres high, protected by immense windbreak walls. There were two tall chimneys and a vast sunken concrete tank which were probably used in manufacturing hydrogen gas for the airships by a process of mixing caustic soda and ferrous iron. A small town consisting of support services, water tanks, gasworks, gasometers, barracks, canteens, a church and a theatre was rapidly constructed to cater for around 500 naval personnel based there.

Huge concrete mooring blocks were used to anchor the airships, dubbed 'Lenabo soos' by the local farmers. Landing the airships involved everyone on the base – even the station dog was trained to assist by grabbing the end of the landing cable which, when thrown from the airship, inevitably landed in a tangled heap. The cable was passed through an iron ring on a vast concrete block to prevent the airship from rising again. These concrete blocks can still be seen half buried in the undergrowth which now covers the site.

Even in good weather conditions 100 naval ratings were needed to manoeuvre the airships into the sheds by hauling on the landing cable, an almost impossible task in bad weather. Each ship had an emergency panel which could be activated to deliberately rip the casing causing the gas to escape and the ship to collapse. On 21 September 1918 two coastal airships landed in a gale; even with 400 men on the ropes it was impossible to get the airships into the sheds under such conditions and they had to be deliberately ripped.

Even though some of the later airships were capable of being airborne for up to 40 hours, their actual effectiveness is very much open to question. However the presence of airships able to protect the merchant ship convoys sailing round the north east coast probably acted as deterrent to the U-boat patrols. Towards the end of the war Lenabo airships protected vessels laying nets armed with mines across routes thought to be used by enemy submarines.

Airships themselves were vulnerable to attack from enemy gunners. Airship C25 was lost at sea off Rattray Head after such an attack in July 1918. A few days after the disappearance its wooden propeller was found at sea and returned to Lenabo where, after being inscribed with the names of the crew, it was displayed in the wardroom. The propeller was later put on display in St John the Evangelist Episcopal Church in Longside where it remains.

In 1919 NS11, the last airship to fly from Lenabo, won a world endurance record for a flight of 100 hours and 50 minutes but was later lost at sea.

Interest in airships generally declined after the war ended and Lenabo was decommissioned in 1920, the railway line was removed in 1923. Now only the concrete bases, windbreaks and larger chunks of concrete masonry remain half concealed, eerily in the undergrowth of what is now mature woodland. In 2003 a memorial plaque to all who served at the base was erected by Longside Community Council on what is believed to be a chimney stack surviving from the officers' mess. Lenabo personnel are also commemorated on the memorial cairn at the nearby RAF Peterhead Airfield.

Rora Moss (NK 056 485): Rora moss, a raised bog area now a Site of Special Scientific Interest, has long provided peat for domestic fuel. Until the latter part of the 20th century whole families would be involved in the summer in the backbreaking work of cutting peats, stacking and turning them to dry on the moss before carting the dried peats home to be stacked and used as winter fuel. Peat cutting competitions were sometimes held on the moss. The *Peterhead Sentinel* reports that at one such event in June 1860, *'Two sturdy candidates attended by a buxom damsel to empty barrows, cast 180 barrowfuls at 12 peats per barrow in an hour'*. Commercial peat extraction, largely for horticultural use, continues on the moss.

The RAF Memorial at Longside Airfield

Longside airfield.   *(Cabro Aviation Ltd)*

As this traditional rhyme records the meandering North and South Ugie Waters, join in Rora Moss:

> *Little Ugie said to Muckle Ugie*
> *'Where shall we meet?'*
> *'Doon in the Haughs of Rora*
> *When man is asleep.'*

The confluence of the rivers was said to be the haunt of a kelpie and it was here that until the early 20th century the nomadic Stewart family regularly fished for pearls. They used a small boat, holding a glass bottomed bucket over the side to see the large mussel shells on the river bed. Huge piles of empty shells were discarded on the river banks. Permit holders still fish the Ugie for salmon and sea trout.

The Pitfour Canal, an abortive attempt by James Ferguson of Pitfour to construct a waterway from the sea to his estate, reaches inland to the haughs of Rora ending abruptly near Artlaw.

According to *The Howes o' Buchan*, the Line crosses the Ugie by, *'a handsome metal bridge of three spans with metal girders, the arches being about eighteen feet apart, and the piers of solid masonry...The view of Rora obtained from the Line at this point is a most enchanting one. The fields arrayed in their thick mantle of living green, all tend at once to gratify the sense and charm the eye by their silent suggestions of honest plenty and well rewarded toil.'*

Longside (Peterhead) Airfield (NK 075 473): Officially known as RAF Peterhead, this Second World War airfield which opened in July 1941 was built on land compulsorily purchased from the Buthlaw Estate by the Air Ministry, with payment deferred until after the war. There were three runways and over 1,800 personnel were housed in accommodation huts dispersed round the east and south east of the airfield.

The threat of invasion by the enemy was thought to be very real so air force personnel were trained to help repel invaders on the ground, airmen were given training in bayonet fighting and officers were trained in the use of Tommy guns. In order that all personnel could have some form of weapon pikes were especially manufactured for use as makeshift bayonets. Hardly high tech weaponry! The airfield was also defended by four Bofors guns and was frequently attacked by enemy planes.

 Peterhead became a very busy airfield with the specific function of accommodating fighter

Newseat in September 2009. In the 1980s the building was roofless but it was rebuilt as a modern home in 1989.

(Keith Fenwick)

squadrons, chiefly Spitfires, Mustangs and Beaufighters for convoy and patrol duties in addition to guarding Britain against attack. Part of the role of the base was to provide fighter protection for aircraft from Banff Strike Wing which, by late 1944, were heavily involved in attacking German shipping off Norway.

The airfield played a part in Operation Tindall during the summer of 1943 when, in order to give enemy reconnaissance aircraft the impression that British and American forces were gathering in preparation for an attack on Norway, dummy aircraft, a camp and gun emplacements were positioned round the base for a time. Similarly, in April 1944, during Operation Fortitude, the false impression of a build-up of aircraft in the North East in preparation for an invasion of Norway was created, this time to detract the Germans from the Normandy Beaches during the D-Day landings.

A Longside locum, Doctor Garden, who carried out medical duties at the aerodrome, was found to be acting as a German spy and was imprisoned.

Military flying ended in August 1945 but the airfield remained the property of the Air Ministry until 1959. It was used as a heliport for several years but is now used by micro lights and light aircraft and for the storage of oil related equipment.

Longside Cemetery contains 19 War Graves which include several RAF personnel and aircrews who died whilst based at Longside. On 14 September 2003 the Longside branch of the British Legion erected a granite memorial cairn to those who served at the airfield during the Second World War. This is easily accessible and is situated just off the A950 Longside to Peterhead road close to the Buthlaw turn off.

Inverugie station in September 1953. The neat station building, with its crow-stepped gables, dates from the 1880s.

(John A N Emslie)

Newseat Station (NK 078 480): This isolated station served the nearby farms and Bruthlaw Estate and quickly established itself as a favourite dropping off point for Peterhead fishwives. Carrying creels of fresh fish they would catch the morning train to Newseat and spend the day walking from door to door through the countryside bartering their fish for produce such as butter and eggs. During the Second World War, Newseat was the station used by personnel from RAF Peterhead.

Inverugie (NK 101 481): A charming description of life in the hamlet of Inverugie is given in *Ugie Pearls* by Winnie Carnegie who spent her childhood there in the interwar years. Although much changed Inverugie remains an attractive mile long ribbon of dwellings stretching down towards the old station from the ruined castle. It is still easy to see why, in less ambitious days, Inverugie, with its tennis courts and charming woodlands, was such a mecca for 'Toonsers' from Peterhead. Visitors cycled or took the train to enjoy days out in the village, picnicking and gathering the wild flowers, snowdrops, primroses and wild honeysuckle in St Johns Wood where, on local holidays, stalls sold such delights as lucky tatties and ice cream.

The railway played a significant part in providing postal services. Mail was carried by train and several stations acted as post offices. Today all that is left are a few post boxes, such as this one at Inverugie.

Inverugie Station (NK 097 474): *Ugie Pearls* gives a vivid description of the village station and the pride in its upkeep taken by the Station Master, Mr Gauld, and the station staff. The station was enhanced by the flowers – asters, marigolds and antirrhinums which they grew on the bank opposite – earning several best kept station awards. On the platform there were colourful enamel advertising signs for Lipton's Tea, Tyler Boots and Monkey Brand Soap – and a slot machine dispensing very small bars of chocolate. Posters in the waiting room advertised what are tellingly described as, '*faraway places such as Edinburgh or Glasgow.*'

Inverugie Castle (NK 102 483): This once palatial castle perched defensively high on the steep bank of the River Ugie was built by the Cheynes but the estate of Inverugie subsequently passed to the vastly wealthy Keiths, Earl Marischals of Scotland. In 1587 George Keith, 4th Earl Marischal, was granted the right to establish a Burgh of Barony three miles from Inverugie at Keith Inch. From a small fishing village this rapidly expanded to become Peterhead, one of Scotland's premier fishing ports. In 1593 George Keith founded Marischal College in Aberdeen.

The ruins of Inverugie Castle still convey a sense of its former elegance. When the Earl Marischal returned to Scotland following his exile he rode out to view the remains of the castle by then 'a desolate ruin' and was so distressed by what he saw that he never returned to his former seat. The castle grounds contain what is thought to have been one of the earliest ice houses in Scotland.

The Keiths forfeited their estates following the Jacobite rising of 1715 when both George Keith, Earl Marischal, and his younger brother James Francis Edward, later to become Field Marshal Keith, supported the Jacobite cause. It was at the Earl Marischal's behest that on 23 September 1715, the Old Pretender, after whom James Keith had been named, was proclaimed King James VIII at the Old Market Cross in Peterhead. After forfeiture the estate was bought by the York Building Company but the Dowager Lady Marischal was permitted to continue living in impoverishment in the castle which began to fall into disrepair. Her two sons escaped to France and subsequently had distinguished military careers, including participation in the abortive 1719 Jacobite Rising.

Following the Dowager's death in 1729 the castle was looted and the York Building Company ran into financial difficulties. The estate was back on the market by 1763 by which time the Earl Marischal's attainder had been reversed and he was able to buy back part of his lost estate. In 1766 Inverugie was sold to James Ferguson of Pitfour who added floors and a roof to the ruin intending to use it as an observatory. Unfortunately, in May 1825 in order to avoid paying rates on it, James Fergusson's nephew George, who had succeeded him, stripped and blew up part of the castle. George Ferguson was also responsible for having a panel bearing the Earl Marischal's coat of arms removed from above the gateway to the castle courtyard and placed on top of the Reform Monument in Broad Street, Peterhead.

Around 1819 a small brewery was operated in part of the ruins by a Mr Sellar. The ruins suffered considerable damage during gales in 1890 and again on New Year's Day 1899 so that, in the interests of safety, they were partially demolished by being blown up. The castle is now fenced off and is inaccessible to the public.

Some sources (including Tayler *Jacobites of Aberdeenshire and Banffshire in the Rising of 1715*) mention the conjecture that it was in the formal gardens at Inverugie that Robert Burnes, (sic) grandfather of the poet, Robert Burns, trained as a gardener and that he came 'out' with the Earl Marischal in the '15. Elsewhere William Burnes, father of Robert Burns, is cited as the gardener.

Ravenscraig Castle (NK 095 487): Also known as the Craig of Inverugie, Ravenscraig was named for the ravens which nested there. Built on a precipitous rock on the bank of the Ugie

Peterhead looking east. The trackbed runs right of centre through the photograph.

(Cabro Aviation Ltd)

Peterhead Power Station. (Cabro Aviation Ltd)

the ruins of the massive four storey L-plan tower are now shrouded by trees. The vaulted ground floor remains but over the centuries the tower has been badly denuded of its decorative features. The present castle is thought to date from about 1491 although an earlier castle on the site is said to have been visited by Robert the Bruce in 1308. The castle was the seat of the barony of Torthorston, originally a Cheynes stronghold, which passed to the Keiths, Earl Marischals, in the mid-14th century. It was also said to have been visited by James VI in 1598 when he was a guest at the marriage of the Laird's daughter.

Castlehill of Inverugie (NK 102 486): Sometimes referred to as Hangman's Hill of Inverugie, this was the site of an earthwork castle built by the Cheynes in the 13th century. The conspicuous motte, on the summit of the hill and now about 3 metres high, would originally have been accompanied on the west side by a bailey, traces of which show up in aerial photographs.

Mount Pleasant (NK 100 477): It is claimed that much of the Keith's family silver was buried in a field at Mount Pleasant to prevent it being confiscated when Inverugie was forfeited after the 1715 Jacobite rising. During the Second World War, Peterhead Auxiliary Patrol's concealed Operational Base was located in a sloping field at Mount Pleasant close to Inverugie Station. The beaches north of Peterhead were considered to be likely sites for the landing of invading troops and the Patrol's targets if invasion had occurred included RAF Peterhead (Longside), road bridges over the River Ugie and the railway to Maud and Peterhead.

Katteburn (NK 102 472): A high red brick wall bounds the extensive garden of Katteburn, which is described in *The Howes o' Buchan* as *'Lying in the hollow, on the right of the line, (approaching Inverugie from Peterhead) Katburn Cottage, with its beautiful, tasteful, and neatly laid off garden, will claim the attention of all passers-by. The cottage is occupied by William Mitchell, Esq., ship owner, Peterhead as a summer residence. Lying as it does in the hollow sheltered by trees, and surrounded by many objects of natural beauty, it forms in itself quite a little paradise.'*

Peterhead Power Station (NK 127 431): The power station became operational in 1980 and is described by Charles McKean as *'Power with cleanliness realised in architecture: the massing of simple blocks focused on a tall chimney stack lends coherence and geometry to the messy complications of electricity generation'*. The power station, currently owned by Scottish and Southern Energy plc, employs about 160 workers and has the capacity to produce electricity from either oil or gas depending on which is the most economical. The Peterhead Carbon Capture Scheme is planned to capture up to 10 million tonnes of carbon dioxide emissions which will be piped out for storage under the North Sea.

Howe O' Buchan level crossing. Once well outside Peterhead, the trackside is now increasingly built up.

Howe O' Buchan (NK 106 464): The present Howe O' Buchan house was built around 1840-5 but has the date stone of an earlier house which stood behind it, inscribed 'A S W J S 1711', above the front door. The house contains a sculptured panel and bannisters which originated in Brucklay Castle.

By 1853 Howe O' Buchan was the home of Thomas Walker, one of four brothers whose family had originated at Waulkmill and Bankhead in New Aberdour and who between them owned the neighbouring estates of Richmond, Balmore Grange and Howe O' Buchan. When the railway station opened in Peterhead the water needed for the engines was pumped from there.

Meethill Reform Tower (NK 122 446): The Reform Tower was built in 1832, on the site of a prehistoric burial cist, by the local Whig (now Liberal) Party to celebrate the introduction of the Parliamentary Reform Act of 1832. This made Peterhead a Parliamentary Burgh and gave all male householders whose property had an annual value of £10 or more the right to vote. The 5 storey granite tower, in plan a Greek cross, was originally intended to be an observatory. According to local traditions a child met his death by falling from the tower which also once provided a hiding place for an escaped prisoner.

Peterhead Station (NK 127 466): Nothing now remains of Peterhead Station; the site has been redeveloped and forms part of the campus for Peterhead Academy and Community Centre.

When the Station opened in 1862 it was situated on the western outskirts of the town, surrounded by open countryside. *Howes o' Buchan* describes how the traveller could look out of the carriage window at *'a broad expanse of Ocean, Rattray Head appearing in full relief... close to the sea in the hollow the little village of Buchanhaven ... Close to the station on the left is the Washing House Croft occupied by Mr Charles Will 'chemist', his chemistry is pretty much confined to the distillation of aromatic essences from sweet herbs such as peppermint etc...before his door is the Washing House Green, used by the inhabitants generally for bleaching their clothes'.* During the 17th century unfortunates accused of witchcraft were burned at the stake on the green.

The peripheral location of the station soon proved to be inconvenient for the amount of goods traffic generated by the port so a line was built to the harbour in 1865. This closed in 1939.

The arrival of the railway introduced the electric telegraph to Peterhead and revolutionised mail delivery. In 1824 the mail coach *The Earl of Erroll* covered the journey from Aberdeen to Peterhead in five hours and could carry a dozen passengers, four of whom were able to travel inside the coach, the rest enduring a cold and uncomfortable journey outside. Sandy Scott, the Peterhead mail carrier from about 1825 to 1865, began his rounds by going to the foot of the Tory Reform Monument and handing out letters to folk congregating there who expected mail. In 1896 the mail left Aberdeen by train at 8.05 a.m., reaching Fraserburgh and Peterhead at 9.55 a.m. in time to go out on the second delivery of the day.

The last train at Peterhead in 1970 was a special from Aberdeen organised to mark the event. The station had already been cleared of wagons. The signal arms were removed some years before, but the posts remained and proved irresistible to photographers who wanted to obtain a good view of the area. The passenger station can be seen in the centre with the extensive goods yard to the left. Off picture to the left were the locomotive shed and the line to the harbour.   *(Mike Stephen)*

As in Fraserburgh, fishing generated huge amounts of traffic for the railway, not only outgoing fish but also incoming oil and coal for the drifters, the coal originating in the Fife coal fields, vast amounts of ice and salt for preserving the fish and general stores for the boats. During the 1950s and 60s empty tin cans were sent by train to Peterhead from the Metal Box factory at Arbroath then returned south full of Crosse & Blackwell's products.

Between 1871 and 1916 the Great North of Scotland Granite Company operated a granite polishing works close to the station. The works specialised in the production of high quality stone used by monumental masons in Britain and abroad and for the ornamental frontages of buildings such as the Foreign Office in London.

Peterhead Academy (NK 127 464): The oldest part of the buildings dates from 1890, when girls were admitted for the first time, but has been extended on several occasions to provide modern educational facilities in a building which has the largest floor space of any school in Scotland. On 31 January 1922 the back part of the building was destroyed by fire, and the building was twice damaged during air raids in 1940, giving pupils an extended summer break. Appropriately for a school located close to a former granite works the school motto is '*Domus Super Petram Aedificata*' which translates as 'A House Built On A Rock'.

Peterhead (NK 132 462): The most easterly town in Scotland, Peterhead has grown from its foundation on Inch Keith by George Keith, 4th Earl Marischal in 1587 to become the largest town in Aberdeenshire, having a population of 18,500. As befits a town whose name is probably derived from the Gaelic, *Pett-air-Usige*, meaning 'Town on the water', Peterhead has capitalised on its maritime heritage achieving pre-eminence at various times as a sealing and whaling port, the UK's largest white fish and pelagic port and oil supply base, and is now visited by cruise ships. The oldest building in Peterhead, Ugie Smokehouse, dating from 1585, produces locally caught gourmet smoked salmon and is reputedly the oldest working premises in Scotland.

Peterhead was once the leading whaling port in Great Britain and exploited stormy whaling grounds including the Greenland Sea and Davies Straits. Established around 1788, the fleet grew to 31 ships by the mid-1850s. In 1823 alone 268 whales were killed for their blubber which was used to provide oil for candles and oil lamps. Whaling was both extremely lucrative and extremely dangerous, carrying high risk of an unsuccessful trip. Voyages often lasted for months, conditions on board the ships were harsh, many lives were lost and ships could be trapped and crushed in pack ice. Small boats were used to chase and harpoon the whales which were flensed in the sea before the blubber was hauled onto the main boat to be stored in barrels for the return voyage. Thousands of people were employed in associated trades such as provisioning and equipping the whalers and boiling up the blubber in the boilyards on Inch Keith. The industry lasted for about a century by which time the whale population was reduced and shale oil was available for lighting.

The decline in whaling coincided with the rise of herring fishing, by 1890 there were around 600 vessels fishing from Peterhead. Vast amounts of herring were exported but a considerable volume was canned there. Peterhead has been associated with fish canning since 1850, when Ritchie & Co. established a food preserving company which began by preserving salmon and tongue partly

The bronze cast of 'Fisher Jessie', a creel carrying fish–wife, and her daughter reflects Peterhead's pride in its fishing heritage.

to supply the whalers. Later the plant was taken over by Crosse & Blackwell who eventually diversified from fish canning to processing a wide range of foods, the smell of the most pungent, Branston Pickle, often pervading the town before the factory closed in 1998.

The strategic position of Peterhead for vessels seeking shelter from the perilous North Sea led to the decision in 1886 to provide a harbour of refuge. Granite from Stirling Quarry and precast concrete blocks each weighing 40 tons were used to construct two massive protecting breakwaters encompassing an area of 300 acres. Peterhead Prison was built to provide the convict labour needed for the quarry and workshop where the stone was dressed and a railway line, then the only state owned passenger line in Britain, was laid to transport prisoners securely. Warders armed with cutlasses guarded the convicts as they were transported from the Admiralty Yard by the prison, where materials were stored, to the granite quarry at Stirling Hill and the workshop. The project, delayed by winter storms, ran vastly over budget and was only completed in truncated form in the late 1950s. By the time of completion the demise of sailing ships meant that there was little need for the harbour of refuge but with the discovery of North Sea oil and gas it found a new role in servicing the industry.

Proclamation Pend (NK 133 461): On 21 August 1715, at the Tolbooth near the south end of Broad Street, George Keith, Earl Marischal proclaimed James Francis Stuart, father of Bonnie Prince Charlie, as rightful king of Scotland. Nearby Proclamation Pend commemorates this historic event, one of several proclamations in

the North East which, along with the raising of the Standard of King James VIII at Braemar by the Earl of Mar on 6 September, was effectively the start of the 1715 Jacobite campaign. Following the example of the laird, there was strong support for the Jacobites in the burgh. The arrangements to defend the town for the Jacobites included the mounting of Spanish guns on the Tolbooth Green and the drawing up of lists of those inhabitants, including some women, who were obliged to carry arms in the town's defence. Four months later, on the night of 22 December 1715, too late to offer leadership in the faltering campaign, Stuart himself landed clandestinely at Peterhead. The Jacobite campaign was so disastrous that on 4 February 1716 Prince James Francis Stuart fled Scotland from Montrose – two days before the Jacobite troops were disbanded. During this campaign and the '45, Jacobite resources and troops from the continent were smuggled into Scotland through Peterhead.

The Town House (NK 134 461): The Town House, boasting a spire *'in the style of Wren'*, was built of local granite in 1788 on the site of the old Tolbooth but was not fully completed until 1813. The building retained the old prison vaults and has three storeys; until about 1850 there was an arcaded market on the ground floor and the parish school used two rooms on the first floor where there were also council offices. Until 1881, when a porch containing steps was added, the first floor of the building was reached by external steps. Over the years parts of the building have served an astonishing range of unexpected purposes including housing the Post Office and a library, providing a soup kitchen, garaging the fire engine and in 1865 storing the Volunteer Corps' supply of weapons and gunpowder!

Statue of Field Marshal James Keith (NK 134 460): Field Marshal James Francis Edward Keith of Inverugie was born in 1696. Named after James Francis Edward Stuart, the Old Pretender, Keith was born into a strongly Jacobite family. Along with his elder brother George, Earl Marischal, he participated in the unsuccessful risings of 1715 and 1719 after which he was forced into exile on the continent. He then became a mercenary soldier in the Spanish army before, in 1728, entering service in the Russian army and having a hugely successful career, fighting major campaigns in Poland and the Ottoman Empire. In 1747 Keith

Statue of Field Marshal James Keith outside the Town House.

The gold lion rampant on top of the Broad Street Reform Monument symbolises a united Great Britain.

joined the army of Frederick the Great of Prussia, again serving with distinction, rising to the rank of Field Marshal, becoming Governor of Berlin and fighting in the Seven Years War. He lost his life on 14 October 1758 defending the battery of cannon which he commanded in the battle of Hochkirchen. The Broad Street statue of Field Marshal Keith, a replica of a monument in Berlin, was gifted to Peterhead by William I, King of Prussia in August 1868. Field Marshal Keith is still recognised as a hero in former Prussia.

Broad Street Reform Monument (NK 134 461): A year after the building of Meethill Reform Tower the Peterhead Tories also constructed a monument to commemorate the Reform Bill. Situated in Broad Street, this is a single column on a granite base surmounted by four square panels bearing Latin inscriptions, the plant badges of Scotland, Ireland and England, and the arms of the Earl Marischal removed from Inverugie Castle by Captain Ferguson of Pitfour, in turn topped by a Lion Rampant, in gold rather than red, so that it symbolises a united Great Britain.

Old St Peter's Church (NK 126 460): Situated on the braeside overlooking the sea and surrounded by its graveyard, little now remains of the 13th century parish church of St Peter other than the ruined chancel arch and the west bell tower. The square bell tower is thought to date from around 1670 and was kept in good repair after the church was abandoned around 1770. J Findlay, writing in *A History of Peterhead* describes how during the late 18th and early 19th centuries the tower was *'used as a watchtower against the resurrectionists, the relatives of the dead mounted guard over newly buried bodies, and many times at the dead of night has the frenzied clangour of the old bell wakened the inhabitants of the town to tell them that the grave-openers were at their horrible work again.'*

The bell tower in Old St Peter's Church yard was used as a watch tower against grave robbers in the late 18th and early 19th centuries. The graveyard contains many interesting gravestones dating from the 17th century onwards, indicating the commerce and trades with which Peterhead has been associated over the centuries.

Access, Car Parking and Public Transport

The route is clearly defined and provided with information panels at several points. Apart from ramps at some road crossings it involves only very gentle gradients. The path is predominantly gravel with some tarred sections although some stretches, especially in cuttings, can become very muddy. It is suitable for use by walkers of all abilities, cyclists and, away from the urban stretches, horse riders. Dogs should be kept under close control especially near farm animals and during the shooting season. The Formartine and Buchan Way is maintained by Aberdeenshire Council. You can find more details about it at www.aberdeenshire.gov.uk/outdooraccess/long_routes/formartine_buchan.asp.

The Walkhighlands web site has guidance for users, including maps and walking times, at www.walkhighlands.co.uk/aberdeenshire/formartine-buchan-way.shtml.

Dyce is easily reached from Aberdeen by bus or train. Both Fraserburgh and Peterhead have frequent bus services to Aberdeen which pass through Ellon. Buses from Fraserburgh also pass through Strichen and Mintlaw and a frequent service connects Peterhead with Fraserburgh. There is no direct public transport link between Peterhead and Maud but a limited bus services links Maud with Fraserburgh, Auchnagatt, Ellon and Aberdeen. There is a frequent service between Newmachar, Dyce and Aberdeen. Public transport arrangements are, of course, subject to change. For transport between intermediate points please check at www.aberdeenshire.gov.uk/publictransport/.

Main access points where there is official car parking are listed below. It is usually also possible to park a single car safely on the verge at many of the road crossings where care should be taken to avoid blocking agricultural access. Access to the Line from roads which pass over it is frequently by a very steep embankment or steps.

Various attractions such as museums close to the line are listed inside the rear cover.

Fraserburgh –Maud

Ordnance Survey Explorer Map 427 covers this section

Fraserburgh: Purists will wish to start the walk from the site of the railway station on Station Brae but the walk is signposted from the Beach Esplanade where there is car parking available. There is flat access to the Way at this point.

Strichen: Access from the junction of Bridge Street and Brewery Road close to the entrance to Strichen Community Park. This involves a ramp if heading towards Fraserburgh or steps towards Maud but there is flat access from further west along Brewery Road where there is a small car park. There is car parking at Strichen Community Park and in Market Terrace.

Maud: From the station car park enter the station turn left onto the path and cross over the underpass, noting the Second World War pillbox, almost immediately there is a slight ramp to a road crossing after which the Way continues – signposted Strichen.

Maud – Dyce

Ordnance Survey Explorer Maps 427 and 421 cover this section.

Maud: Car parking at the station which is signposted in the village. From there turn right along the track bed for easy flat access to the Line heading for Auchnagatt.

Auchnagatt: Parking at Auchnagatt Public Hall, access to the Line after crossing the A948.

Ellon: There are several car parks in Ellon. Station Road East is closest to the Line. The Way is accessible from several points on the western side of Ellon including from the paths on both the north and south banks of the Ythan, from Station Road and via a link path from Hospital Road. There is also ramped access from Riverside Road. Caution is needed when crossing the busy A920 south of Ellon.

Udny Station: Parking and access from the recreation park on Chestnut Walk.

Newmachar: Limited car parking to the north of the village close to Newmachar Station. There is flat access at this point.

Dyce: Parking and level access from the north end of Dyce Station.

Maud – Peterhead

Maud: Car parking at the Station. From the station car park either head towards the general store and cross under the Line using the pedestrian under pass which is between the car park and the shop or cross the trackbed and island platform then head down the slope to the left of the station. The Line to Peterhead, signposted Mintlaw, is just ahead on the left side of the road (B9029 – Deer Road East).

Mintlaw: Car parking at the recreation ground next to the garden centre on North Street adjacent to the crossing of the Formartine and Buchan Way with the busy A952, there is a descent to the Line from the road.

Longside: Parking at Main Street in the village. Access to the Way is from Station Road and Station Terrace at Auchlee Bridge, close to the site of the old station to the north of the village centre.

Peterhead: Flat access between two houses on York Street close to the Community Centre where there is car parking. Car parking also available at York Street car park.

At Dyce, the Formartine and Buchan Way starts inconspicuously at the north east end of the car park.

The end of the Way at Peterhead is also not very evident, but at least the vertical sleepers give a clue.

Bibliography

Titles referred to in the text

Anderson, W, *The Howes o' Buchan* (W.P.Nimmo, Lewis Smith, Peterhead Sentinel 1865)

Buchan, A R, *Pitfour, The Blenheim of the North* (The Buchan Field Club 2008)

Cranna, J, *Fraserburgh Past and Present* (Rosemount Press 1914)

Dey, G A, (Ed) *Around the White Horse, From Memoirs by Mrs C. J. Thomson* (P. Scrogie Ltd. 1991)

Findlay, J T, *A History of Peterhead From Prehistoric Times to AD 1986* (P Scroggie Ltd & D Wyllie & Son 1933)

McKean, C, *Banff and Buchan an Illustrated Architectural Guide* (Mainstream Publications 1990)

Pratt, Rev. J B, *Buchan* (Heritage Press 1978)

Pratt, Rev J.B, *Jamie Fleeman, The Laird of Udny's Fool* (Heritage Press 1980)

Presslie W, (Ed I W Platt) *The Uncommon Herd* (Digital Print Media, 2012) Autobiography of William Presslie

Tayler, A & H, *Jacobites of Aberdeenshire and Banffshire in the Forty-Five* (Milne & Hutchison 1928)

Tayler, A & H, *Jacobites of Aberdeenshire and Banffshire in the Rising of 1715* (Oliver and Boyd 1934)

Temple, Rev W, *The Thanage of Fermartyn* (D Wyllie and Son 1894)

Wilken, J, *Ellon in Bygone Days* (P.Scrogie 1921)

Further Reading : General Histories of Aberdeenshire

Alexander, W, *Place Names of Aberdeenshire* (Aberdeen Spalding Club 1952)

Buchan, J, *Bygone Buchan* (The Buchan Field Club 1987)

Chorlton, M, *Scottish Airfields in the Second World War Vol.3 The Grampians* (Countryside Books 2010)

Fenwick, Flett and Jackson, *Railways of Buchan*, (GNSRA, 2008)

Hamilton H, (Ed) *Third Statistical Account of Scotland –The County of Aberdeen* (Collins 1960)

Sangster, A H, *The Story and Tales of the Buchan Line* (Oxford Publishing Co.1983)

Shepherd, I A G, *Exploring Scotland's Heritage: Grampian* (HMSO 1986)

Smith, R, Buchan, *Land of Plenty* (John Donald Publishers Ltd.1996)

Thomas, J, and Turnock, D, *Regional History of Railways of Great Britain, Vol 15 North of Scotland,* (House of Lochar, 1989)

Tocher, J F, *The Book of Buchan* (The Buchan Club 1910)

Wood, S, *The Shaping of 19th Century Aberdeenshire* (SPA Books 1985)

Fraserburgh to Maud

Buchan, J, *Bygone Fraserburgh* (Stenlake Publishing) 2002

Fraser, F M, 20th Lady Saltoun, *Clan Fraser, A History* (Scottish Cultural Press 1997)

Jack, R A, *Maud, A Glimpse into the Past* (W Peters & Son Ltd 1986)

Murison, D, *The Broch as it Was* (D Urquhart, 1991)

Murison, D, & Noble, L, *Names and Places, A history of place and street names in and around Fraserburgh* (Buchan Publishing, 1995)

Oram R D, Martin P F, McKean C A, Neighbour T, Cathcart A, *Historic Fraserburgh Archaeology and Development* (Council for British Archaeology and Historic Scotland 2010)

Maud to Dyce

Birnie, L, *Old Ellon* (Stenlake Publishing 2005)

Ord, C.W. *Dyce, A Historical Miscellany of An Aberdeenshire Parish* (Aberdeen and North East Family History Society 2004)

Penny, C, (Ed) *Stuartfield, Our Place* (Stuartfield Millennium Group 2000)

Shepherd, I A G, *Aberdeenshire: Donside and Strathbogie: An Illustrated Architectural Guide* (The

Rutland Press 2006)

Toulmin, D, *The Tillycorthie Story* (The Centre for Scottish Studies, University of Aberdeen 1986)

Wilken, J, *Ellon in Bygone Days* (P.Scrogie 1921)

Maud to Peterhead

Bertie, D M, *History of Longside Episcopal Church 1992* (David Bertie 1992)

Coull, S, *Nothing But My Sword* (Birlinn 2000) – The life of Field Marshal James Keith

Ellsworth, R and Beresford Ellis, P, *The Book of Deer* (Library of Celtic Illuminated Manuscripts, Constable 1994)

Elphinstone. K, *Deer Parish Church 200 Years On* (P.Scrogie Ltd. 1989)

May, Violet and Alexander, *Longside a parish and its people* (Longside Parish Church 2000)

Useful Websites

canmore.rcahms.gov.uk : The Royal Commission on the Ancient and Historic Monuments of Scotland contains site records for the national collection of buildings, archaeology and industry.

www.coleshillhouse.com : Coleshill Auxiliary Research Team (CART) records relating to the British Resistance.

www.gnsra.org.uk : Great North of Scotland Railway Association.

maps.nls.uk : National Library of Scotland map collection including historic Ordnance Survey maps, aerial photographs and a wealth of earlier maps.

www.scotlandsplaces.gov.uk : search by place across national data bases of historical records including records held by the National Library of Scotland and the National Records of Scotland.

edina.ac.uk/stat-acc-scot : online version of the Statistical Account of Scotland 1791 – 99 and New Statistical Account of Scotland 1845. Compiled by parish ministers, these contain detailed first hand contemporary accounts of life in each parish.

The formal opening of the Formartine and Buchan Way took place on 25 September 2013 at Maud. The ribbon was cut by Councillor Jill Webster, Provost of Aberdeenshire and the event was attended by a large group of children from Maud School who planted primrose and harebell 'plugs' beside the path on its way to Strichen. Although much of the Way had been open for many years, this ceremony marked the completion of the final section, from Maud to Strichen. *(Des Byrne)*

Index

Great North of Scotland Railway Association

Founded 1964

The Association caters for all those interested in the history of the Great North of Scotland Railway and its constituent companies, as well as the lines during the LNER, British Railways and post-privatisation periods. The Association promotes the study and collection of information, documents and illustrations relating to all aspects of the North East's railways. It also facilitates and co-ordinates members' research and provides information for modellers.

Members receive a quarterly *Review* containing articles, photographs, drawings and news of the railway, both historical and current. The Association has produced a comprehensive range of books and technical papers covering aspects of the railway in great detail. Members have access to an extensive photographic and drawing archive. Members receive a discount on Association publications. Meetings and excursions are regularly organised.

For further information, please look at the Association's website
www.gnsra.org.uk.